Managing Youth Services

Editors:
Michael Airs
County Youth Officer, Bedfordshire, and
formerly Chairperson, National Association of Youth
and Community Education Officers

Francis Cattermole
Director, National Council for Voluntary
Youth Services

Don Grisbrook
Director, Council for Education and
Training in Youth and Community Work

Longman

Longman Group UK Limited
Longman House, Burnt Mill, Harlow, Essex, CM20 2JE

© Longman Group UK Limited, 1987

First published 1987

British Library Cataloguing in Publication Data
Managing Youth Services
1. Social work with youth ——— Great
Britain
I. Cattermole, Francis   II. Airs, M.
III. Grisbrook, Don
362.7'0941   HV1441.G7

ISBN 0-582-02243-6

Printed in Great Britain by
Page Bros (Norwich) Ltd

Contents

Acknowledgements

The Authors and Publishers wish to thank the following for permission to reproduce copyright materials:

The National Youth Bureau, for permission to reproduce an extract from *Expenditure on Youth Services*;

Croner Publications Ltd., Croner House, 173 Kingston Rd., New Malden, Surrey KT3 3SS, for material used from *The Heads' Legal Guide*;

National Association of Youth Clubs, for an extract from *Girls' Night*;

National Association of Head Teachers for advice contained in Council Memorandum on *Alcohol, Drug and Solvent Abuse*.

Foreword

This book is described as being about "managing the Youth Services". This could be misleading. In our language management is a word with hierarchical overtones. It is often assumed to describe the activities of Top People, who sit in offices and give orders, of planners and policy-makers, and in short of "managers" as distinct from those who are "managed".

There are no doubt some spheres of human activity where this is indeed how matters are arranged – rather like an eighteenth century army. But increasingly in all types of enterprise, and especially in those which depend primarily on human resources, management means something different. It denotes a particular way of addressing a task, and it applies to every level of the system.

We seem not to have an adequate word for this methodology. The first chapter of this book contains a full anatomy of it: more briefly, the Review Group on the Youth Service distinguished four basic components – identifying objectives, assigning roles, allocating resources, and monitoring performance. It is necessary for everyone at every level of a system to do these things to some degree and in one way or another. It should be everyone's aim to do them more consciously, more effectively and more thoroughly.

Systems which operate in this way are organic rather than mechanical. The members of it are not cogs but cells. The management function is not confined to specialist cells (such as management committees or principal officers), but is required also of all those who are misleadingly called the "Rank and File" (an eighteenth century army image). What is being aimed at is nothing less than the full mobilisation of all the human resources available, and that can be achieved only by practising the techniques illustrated in this book.

This is a big claim, but I believe that "management" in this special, pervasive sense is desperately lacking in our society. Maybe the lack of an accepted word for this activity is symptomatic of a wide-spread conceptual failure which may have more to do with our national performance than is generally recognised. It is heartening and fitting that the process should be exemplified in a book about the Youth Services, on which the future of our society will critically depend.

ALAN THOMPSON
Chairman of the Review Group on the Youth Service in
England 1980–82

1 Introduction

Michael Airs and Francis Cattermole

'The overall aims of the youth service should be seen as affirming an individual's self-belief and encouraging participation in society' – *The Thompson Report*

Young people in society

There was a time when a child grew up alongside its parents, learning from them the skills which would enable the family to produce food, to clothe itself and to barter for other goods necessary for the maintenance of life. When the child was capable of acting without the support of its parents and other adults from the extended family, it had become an adult itself.

The coming of an industrial society has created the phenomenon of youth. For many years youth was defined as the period of transition from childhood to adulthood, and the disturbing nature of that transition given as the excuse for the turmoil of adolescence. Today's world sees that period of adolescence itself extended so that youth becomes a time of its own, with psychologists noting the turmoil at the transition from childhood to adolescence (puberty), and from adolescence to adulthood (the young adult).

There is no clear definition of the period of youth, but we are assuming an approximate span from 12 to 25 years – a time starting with secondary education, and continuing until further or higher education, training or work experience for many (but still not all) leads to working life. The period of time has always been one focussed upon by society-watchers. Recently the inhabitants of the age-band have changed from supposed liberators of the world (the 1960's) to the perceived causes of the world's problems (the 1980's). Society changes, and so do the needs of young people within it.

The problem for young people today is that there is no agreed role for them to fulfil. Very few are called upon to leave school and go straight into work. Many are trained for work in the future, but that training brings nothing like universal employment to its graduates. Some maintain a place in formal education long after their peers, but often with little concept of what that education is for. We prepare young people for working life, but there is not enough work for them to do. We admit that work patterns will change, but we cannot say what they will become, or what preparation is needed for the new industrial environment.

Society denies young people a proper place within it – not because it is against young people, but because it does not know what to offer. Thus those adults in society responsible for young people – most notably their parents – are left in the lurch by their adult peers. We do not know what to do with young people, so there is no way they can please us except by keeping quiet and out of the way. Yet it is not that easy. We have tried to develop a form of education that values the inquisitive and enquiring mind, and that tries to encourage participation on the part of young people. We cannot be surprised if they feel a sense of frustration and confusion, in a world which neither they nor anyone else can control any more, and for which it is thus difficult to feel any responsibility.

Against such a background, it is inevitable that work with young people is highlighted by the context of a wide range of social issues. In a book on managing youth services it is not appropriate to address these in detail, but we must register that they are the environment in which the youth service operates.

Young people are both concerned about and affected by the great inequalities that exist in our society. They know of the 'North-South divide' – both as it separates the nations of the world and the people of Britain. They experience a society in which the rich get richer and the poor get poorer. They know that many experience prejudice and discrimination on the grounds of their race or sex. They see political extremism, and as the militants and the fascists recruit from their number, the majority reject political solutions to issues and are apathetic about our democratic institutions.

Some young people, regardless of sex or race, experience particular problems in a confused and confusing society. Many know the ravages of unemployment, either to themselves or to their families. Some are homeless, or experience great difficulty in finding somewhere to live. Some express their contempt for what society has to offer them by turning to crime, and then become even more alienated by the criminal justice system. Some opt out of society in another way, hiding behind drugs, solvents and other mind-numbing substances. Just occasionally a group vents its frustration in violence and riot.

Yet the scenario for young people is by no means all one of doom and gloom. Anybody who has worked with them for long, senses the expectation and hope that is to be found beyond all the odds. The many adults who voluntarily give of their time to work with the young are proof that young people are not wholly cast aside by society. For many young people now there are more opportunities available and at a younger age than there were for previous generations, and they are quick to take the chances that come their way.

There is a new pattern of leisure, often involving the day time as well as the evening. There are new patterns of family life which can increase freedom and responsibility. There are demands for provision which must at the same time be cheap yet sophisticated. Somewhere in all this there is a youth service – an informal sector of provision in which young people voluntarily take part – which for many is a vital resource, a lifeline to finding a place and role in life.

The Thompson Report[1] in 1982 reviewed the youth service, and took as its title 'Experience and Participation'. When published it did not win universal acclaim. The liberals thought it bland, the radicals thought it liberal. In the following five years the experiences of young people have become increasingly depressing and the opportunities to participate fully in society fewer and fewer. The Thompson Report now seems radical to the radicals, and some liberals even define it as subversive. With society changing at such a rate, no service for young people can hope to achieve anything positive without very good management. This book could not be more timely.

The youth service

Every society has an arrangement for the care of its young. In the Britain of 150 years ago these formal, mainly educational arrangements began to be complemented by an informal voluntary network of agencies whose main dynamic was social concern and the welfare of the young. As adolescence has been extended, and the function of those voluntary organisations matched by statutory sector provision, the focus has changed to informal education and political literacy. So we can define THE YOUTH SERVICE as:

> a structural arrangement of voluntary and statutory agencies designed to encourage the personal development and social education of young people by a process of experiential learning.

The range of agencies which comprises this arrangement is wide. The Thompson Report[1] identifies a number of important elements: clubs, uniformed groups, projects, church groups, detached work, counselling agencies, youth councils, community-based groups,

community service agencies, play organisations, residential
provision, specialist activity groups, youth wings of political parties,
groups for the handicapped, and school-based organisations. Whilst
most of these have existed for some time, the respective
contributions they make to the whole complexity of the youth
service have changed with the changing nature of society.

In the current service, it is possible to notice the early stages of the
demise of the traditional youth club as a means of delivery. The need
for daytime provision for those with extended periods of non-work
has led to new concepts of programming. The needs and interests of
young people rather than the needs of society are of increasing
importance in defining both the type of youth service curriculum and
its means of delivery. Single-interest groups are adopting youth
service methods in their work. New provision is springing up from
the local community rather than a national agency or county hall
initiative. Work with the younger end of the age-range becomes
increasingly significant as the age of criminality and alienation fall.
Post-16 provision similarly demands attention as the youth
unemployment rate rises.

The consequence to the youth service of the changing needs of
the young people in a changing society giving rise to changing
provision is a growth of professionalisation. By this we do not mean a
growth of paid staff – they are vital, but the vast majority of workers
are still volunteers. Nor do we mean a swing away from voluntary
sector provision – local authorities still deliver but a small part of the
service. What we do mean is a professional approach to youth work
– in the one-night a week club in a drafty hall and in the purpose-built
full-time centre, in the local authority's education department and in
the voluntary organisation's national headquarters. We ask why
society should intervene in the lives of young people, to what
purpose, in what manner, by whom, and with what preparation and
support. These are the questions for the manager.

The youth officer as manager

Responding to the Thompson Report, the Government of the day
issued a Circular – 1/85[2]. It states:

> The Secretary of State therefore wishes to draw attention to the need to
> ensure sound arrangements for the planning, co-ordination and
> management of the youth service, in order to secure the best return for
> young people from existing resources.

The manager has to agree with most of those wishes, but also to
ensure that the resources are adequate to support provision

appropriate for today's young people. It is how these various resources are handled that constitutes the process of management which is the central theme of this book. An early issue of *The Working With Girls Newsletter* (NAYC) defined management as 'using one's resources effectively in order to achieve one's goals'[3] This very effective definition makes it that clear that the constituent elements of management are those of:

- Purpose and direction
- Resources
- Effectiveness

It is important to stress that within this definition, and indeed this book, the traditional concept of management as a male-dominated hierarchical process is not accepted but rather that management applies throughout the service from the voluntary part-time worker undertaking one session a week to the principal officer, whether of a statutory or voluntary agency. It encompasses those who work directly with young people, those who work with communities, those who work with other staff, those concerned with matters of administration and finance and those who are concerned with policy implementation and resources. All who work within the youth service are arguably involved in all five dimensions but this book is aimed *either* at those who have recently moved to a position of having to concentrate primarily on the latter three aspects; that is:

- Staff
- Administration and finance
- Policy and resources

or at those who hope to make a career move to a post which will focus upon these specific dimensions. The following chapters will act as a guide through these tortuous paths and may be used, as any guide, for reference rather than reading in a pre-determined order.

Returning to the definition of management, readers must consider in some detail what is implied within that definition. The infrastructure supporting those three constituent elements named above is:

1. A need clearly to define the tasks that have to be undertaken. This must be by the use of objective criteria rather than a 'gut feeling'.
2. Once satisfied that tasks exist, a manager must carefully identify the parameters of the agency within which the manager operates and which tasks relate to the functions of other

agencies. This is sometimes a painful process of honesty about one's own agency and about oneself.

3. Having isolated the tasks which are appropriate to the agency, the manager has to examine those tasks against both the overall strategy, aims and purposes of the agency, and the undoubted resource constraints under which the agency will inevitably operate, and come to some conclusions about the order of priority to be accorded to the tasks confronting the agency.

4. Once clarity has been reached about priorities within an overall strategy, the manager has to conceive how best to convince other colleagues within the agency, and ultimately those who have the power of decision-making, about both the overall strategy and the priority order of the component parts of the strategy.

5. That achieved, the manager has to exercise the skills of using resources by initially quantifying the resources necessary for the agreed programme and then securing them. The days when additional resources were easily obtained are long gone but this book spends some time examining how resources external to the agency may be attracted. It is much more likely that the manager will be faced with the difficult task of translating priorities into realities through the re-allocation of existing resources.

6. The manager will, for any particular project, have to be satisfied that it is progressing effectively and this will inevitably lead the manager into ensuring that appropriate training, support and supervision of staff is provided.

7. The manager will need to agree in advance with policy-makers and staff the criteria that will be employed to evaluate the project and the process that will be adopted for the evaluation.

8. These criteria and processes, when applied, will lead the manager to consider the future of any particular aspect of provision:

    - Should it be maintained without variation?
    - Should it be maintained in an adjusted form?
    - Should it be transferred to another agency?
    - Should it be terminated?

9. These tasks are not necessarily easy and the conclusions of the evaluation may not be accepted by all but it is the role of the manager to negotiate the implementation of the evaluation.

And thus the process of this cycle starts again.

It is clear that these management tasks must be performed by individuals who not only can apply the necessary skills to them but who also have an understanding of the needs of young people and the ethos of the service's delivery to young people. In theory these are brought together in the person of the YOUTH OFFICER. In reality the newly appointed youth officer is likely to be a highly effective worker with young people who sees career progression through the advisory, wider policy influencing and management roles of the youth officers. Such progression will not necessarily be within the agency in which the worker is employed; there is significant interchange between the voluntary and statutory organisations that work as partners within the youth service.

Note needs to be taken of the fact that these arrangements are not always as neat as indicated in the proceeding paragraphs. The voluntary sector does not always recruit from professionally trained and experienced youth workers and the statutory sector often adds other dimensions to its service to young people, which can be generally called 'community' (even if ill-defined). Neither can it be assumed that a worker of proven skill with young people and with clear management skills will automatically be able to transfer those skills to the post of youth officer.

It is clear that preparation for progression to the post of youth officer is very often opportunistic. Very few staff development policies in either voluntary or statutory agencies prepare workers for this change of role.

Are there common tasks which confront youth officers in first appointments irrespective of the agency in which they are employed? In order to answer this question a number of agencies were approached for the job descriptions of their first level appointments as youth officers. All the agencies responded willingly and thanks are due to:

Voluntary Organisations:
The Young Men's Christian Association (Local General Secretary)
The Scout Association (Field Commissioner)
The National Association of Youth Clubs (County Organizing Secretary)
The Church of England Youth Service (Diocesan Youth Officer)
The National Federation of Young Farmers' Clubs (County Organiser)

Local Authorities: (for Area Youth Officers)
Bedfordshire County Council
Cambridgeshire County Council
Lancashire County Council
City of Newcastle Upon Tyne
Inner London Education Authority

These job descriptions have been analysed and four broad headings identified:

1. Work specific to the agency.
2. Responsibility for staffing.
3. Responsibility for financial matters.
4. Responsibility for development work.

The broad headings have been further broken down into tasks and the charts in Figure 1, 1.1–1.4 on pages 9, 10 and 11 show the way in which voluntary and statutory sectors emphasise these tasks, although individual agencies are not identified. Acknowledgement must be made of the differing ways in which job descriptions express themselves and the recognition that some tasks may not have been made explicit within the descriptions. The analysis reflects what was contained in the descriptions we were given.

It is clear from this analysis that first appointments for youth officers in both statutory and voluntary agencies have much in common in their definition of duties. Matters such as giving policy advice, dealing with administration, servicing committees, advising and supporting staff, budgeting, initiating and encouraging developmental work, being aware of changes in society and youth work responses, and inter-agency liaison show little variation between the employing agencies.

Areas sharing a significant distinction, such as responsibility for interpreting agency policy, public relations, deployment of staff, granting financial aid or advising other agencies, are clearly attributable to the structure of the agency, the management control exerted by the agency and the geographical size of the area covered by a first appointee.

The scope of this book

There are lessons here for training and (particularly for Regional Advisory Councils of Further Education) for planning the in-service training and education of newly appointed or prospective youth officers in the statutory and voluntary sectors. This book cannot substitute for good training, but it is intended to be a helpful manual and stimulator of thought, particularly for new appointees, and also for their managers and trainers; and their colleagues who have been long in post and would benefit from reviewing their practice.

In Chapters two and three, Tony Huntington explores the vital first stage of identifying needs and establishing priorites, whilst Penny Frost outlines the manager's role in designing programmes

Figure 1 – Comparison of elements in the job descriptions of a youth officer between voluntary organisations and local authorities

Key: V Voluntary agencies
/ Statutory agencies

1.1 *Work Specific to the Agency*

```
-----------------------------------------------------------------
Policy Advice           | VVVVV | VVVVV | VVVVV | VVVVV | VVVVV |
                        | ----- | ----- | ----- | ----- | ----- |
                        | ///// | ///// | ///// | ///// |
------------------------| ----- | ----- | ------------
Administration          | VVVVV | VVVVV |
                        | ----- | ----- |
                        | ///// | ///// |
------------------------| ----- | ----- | -----
Service Committees      | VVVVV | VVVVV | VVVVV |
                        | ----- | ----- | ----- |
                        | ///// | ///// | ///// |
------------------------| ----- | ------------
Report Writing          | VVVVV |
                        | ----- | -----
                        | ///// | ///// |
------------------------| ----- | ----- | -----------
Support Member Groups   | VVVVV | VVVVV | VVVVV | VVVVV |
                        | ----- | ------------------
                        | ///// |
------------------------| ----- | -----------
Public Relations        | VVVVV | VVVVV | VVVVV |
                        | -----------------
                        |
------------------------| -----------
Interpret Agency Policy | VVVVV | VVVVV |
                        | -----------
                        |
--------------------------
```

and provision to meet the needs, which leads inevitably to evaluation and re-assessment of priorities.

Youth officers are not appointed in a vacuum and need to operate skillfully with senior, peer and junior staff to achieve their goals. From a community work perspective, this matrix of accountability is explored by Alan Twelvetrees. The specific concern of supporting staff for whom the manager is responsible by training and staff development is then addressed by Malcolm Payne.

One particular aspect of the context in which the youth service operates is the wide range of legal requirements which the officer needs to be aware of, and this is explored by John Wood in Chapter six.

1.2 Responsibility for staffing

```
-----------------------------------
Recruiting          | vvvvv |
                    |-----|-----
                    |//////|//////|
-------------------------|-----|-----|
Leading             | vvvvv | vvvvv |
                    |-----|-----|-----------------
                    |//////|//////|//////|//////|//////|
-------------------------|-----|-----|-----|-----|-----
Advising            | vvvvv | vvvvv | vvvvv | vvvvv |
                    |-----|-----|-----|-----|
                    |//////|//////|//////|//////|
-------------------------|-----|-----|-----------
Training            | vvvvv | vvvvv |
                    |-----|-----|-----------
                    |//////|//////|//////|//////|
-------------------------|-----|-----|-----|-----|
Supporting          | vvvvv | vvvvv | vvvvv | vvvvv |
                    |-----|-----|-----|-----|-----
                    |//////|//////|//////|//////|//////|
-------------------------|-----|-----|-----------
Supervising         | vvvvv | vvvvv |
                    |-----|-----|-----------------
                    |//////|//////|//////|//////|//////|
-------------------------|---------------------------
Deploying           |
                    |----------------------
                    |//////|//////|//////|//////|
-----------------------------------------------------
```

The next four chapters address different aspects of the officer's role in relation to the resources of the youth service. David Smith identifies the wide range of statutory and voluntary providers, and the value of collaboration between them. Chris Tomsett explores financial management, which he sees as requiring clear identification of needs. Roger Casemore raises particular issued concerning short-term projects. Tanner Shields outlines the special perspective of managing a national youth work agency.

Lastly, we try to avoid the officer's trap of committing all our resources and forgetting our own needs, with a chapter by Mike Cox on the support and training of managers.

One book cannot provide solutions for all the problems of the wide range of people employed as youth officers in the statutory and voluntary youth service. It can raise issues, encourage thought and increase recognition by officers in different agencies of their common concerns.

1.3 Responsibility for Financial Matters

```
-----------------------------------
    Budgeting                    |vvvvv |
                                 |----- |
                                 |//////|
-------------------------------- |----- |
    Allocating                   |vvvvv |
                                 |----- |-----
                                 |//////|//////|
-------------------------------- |----- |----- |-----
    Securing                     |vvvvv |vvvvv |vvvvv|
                                 |----- |----- |-----
                                 |//////|
-------------------------------- |----- |
    Granting                     |
                                 |-----------
                                 |//////|//////|
-------------------------------- |----- |----- |-----
    Controlling                  |vvvvv |vvvvv |vvvvv|
                                 |----- |-----------
                                 |//////|
-------------------------------- |----- |
    Advising                     |
                                 |-----------
                                 |//////|//////|
-----------------------------------------
```

1.4 Responsibility for Development Work

```
-----------------------------------------------------
Awareness                |vvvvv |vvvvv |vvvvv |vvvvv|
                         |----- |----- |----- |-----
                         |//////|//////|//////|
------------------------ |---------------- |-----
Liaise with other agencies |vvvvv |vvvvv |vvvvv |vvvvv |
                         |----- |----- |----- |-----------
                         |//////|//////|//////|//////|//////|
------------------------ |----- |----- |----------------
Initiate                 |vvvvv |vvvvv |
                         |----- |----- |
                         |//////|//////|
------------------------ |----- |----- |
Encourage                |vvvvv |vvvvv |
                         |----- |----- |
                         |//////|//////|
------------------------ |-----------
Advise others            |
                         |----------------
                         |//////|//////|//////|
-----------------------------------------------------
```

The better the management of the youth service, the better its provision. The better its provision the better the meeting of young people's needs. For the youth officer that must be the most important concern of all.

References

1. The Thompson Report (1982), *Experience and Participation, the Report of the Review Group on the Youth Service*, Command 8686, HMSO.
2. (1985) *Circular 1/85, the youth service*, Department of Education and Science.
3. (1981) *Working with Girls Newsletter*, National Association of Youth Clubs.

2 Policies, needs and priorities

Tony Huntington

Chapter one identified that the management of the youth services involves many people. Youth officers occupy a unique management position in that they have a wider framework than a youth worker, and work primarily with adults, including elected committees of councillors or volunteers.

Amongst the core functions of a manager's job are decision-making and problem solving. How often have you had to decide which unit or project should have more resources next year? Should you use this particular member of staff in a new work location within your voluntary organisation? How should you spend your time – dealing with more administration or assessing the quality of the work in the field?

Decisions are therefore central to managing. One simple and useful definition of management is 'deciding what to do and getting it done', and that is the first decision a youth service or organisation and its staff have to make. What is the purpose of the organisation or service? What is it we are attempting to do?

It is appropriate to stress that it is necessary, before attempting to identify needs and establish priorities, that each organisation or authority is clear about what the policy is and how it is implemented.

The need for clarity and consensus about policy

On close examination of either a whole service, organisation or unit it is often possible to discover disparity between the work going on and the written statement of policy. Where there is such a disparity it is often because people within the organisation are not aware of the policy, do not understand the need for a close relationship between policy and practice, or resent the constraining effects which the policy exerts on their 'professional' judgement.

The following section defines some key terms (for example, policy, aims, objectives) and demonstrates that clear linkages between these are an essential support to effective management.

Policy

i) It is the overall organisation or authority policy statement that creates the momentum for what happens.

ii) It provides the criteria against which we assess the work going on; that is, it both validates the programme and provides criteria against which the programme can be evaluated and an officer's own performance assessed.

iii) A policy is the result of an amalgam of inputs; for example educational, philosophical, social, ideological, and professional, and thus hopefully is the outcome of a consultative process.

iv) A policy should be dynamic and not static and therefore have a mechanism by which review and subsequent change are possible.

v) The policy is that overarching statement of intent. It should be an enabling statement; i.e. validate the work of a unit and enable the staff involved eventually to produce aims which reflect the policy statement.

The overall organisational or authority policy may call for policies from its constituent units or institutions. Figure 2.1 (above) demonstrates this in the form of an 'umbrella' policy leading to policy statements within units, which in turn produce specific unit/institutional aims (see page 17 below for aims).

Example one

A national voluntary organisation has an overall statement that outlines its purpose and includes a section on its staffing structure and system of support and training.

At a county or regional level the relevant committee and its officers can use that statement to enable it to produce (and validate) a staff training and development policy which would include aims and objectives.

Example two

A County Council has an overall policy statement on equal opportunities. This will provide a basic set of guidelines which

Figure 2.1

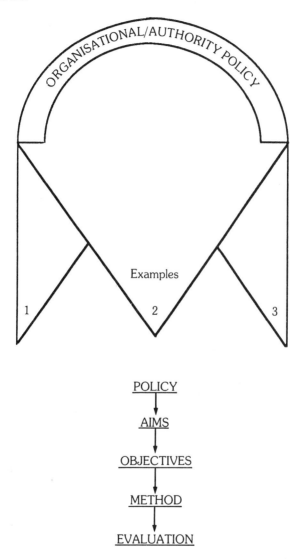

influence and permeate the County Council's work for the public, and is the basis for equal opportunities for the staff working within the County Council.

The County Council's education department will then produce its own policy statement which will reflect not only any national education legislation but also the overall equal opportunity policy of the County Council.

The nature and quality of the education programme will be assessed against, amongst other things, the criteria provided from the equal opportunities policy.

In turn, the policy and practice of a County Council's youth and community service will also be validated by the over-arching policy of the County Council, certainly in respect of equal opportunities, and enable it to describe more focussed aims and objectives.

Example three

Within Derbyshire there is an overall education policy statement, two central characteristics being education for all, and personal and social education.

This in turn provides the general or overarching policy which legitimises and enables the authority's youth and community education service to include the following in its policy statement: that is a broad aim followed by eight objectives (see p 18 for clarification of objectives):

The aim of the Derbyshire youth service is to contribute to the personal and social development of young people within the context of a multi-racial society.

The aim can be achieved by helping young people to:

(1) develop skills to relate effectively with others, and to be effective members of groups in which they live and work.
(2) develop a responsibility towards and a sympathetic concern for other people especially for those who are disadvantaged.
(3) develop decision making skills and political awareness.
(4) adapt and respond to change in themselves and their social and physical environment.
(5) develop confidence in, and an ability to express their own reasoned opinions.
(6) develop an awareness of their own strengths, weaknesses and aptitudes.
(7) develop awareness of their own feelings, attitudes and values as well as those of others.
(8) develop desired manipulative and social skills.

These are seen as the vital personal skills which, though often acquired through home, family, school or work, are the particular province of a social education programme.

The work of the youth and community service is based on this programme; its numerous activities are based on one or more aspects of the programme.

Much youth work currently takes place with school-age young people in institutional settings, working through conventional club activities in school premises or youth service buildings. It is valuable work, and appreciated by those who participate. It is another thing, however, from considering and providing for the needs of those who may have left school perhaps alienated from it, who may be facing unemployment. This will require new resources, a new approach, and a willingness to work with young people where they are to be found in informal and non-institutional settings.

Within the context of the overall policy statement there should be explicit commitments to developing innovative practice and:

- Work with unemployed young people
- Work with girls
- Work with black young people
- Anti-racist work
- Anti-sexist work
- Political education
- Work with young people with special needs

The authority is committed to this policy and looks to all to ensure a more dynamic and relevant service for young people.

The examples given hopefully exemplify the need for a closely stated and understood policy statement which embraces the five policy characteristics given at the start of this chapter. Point number five referred to the policy statement enabling aims to be identified.

Aims

i) Are those statements made which reflect the organisation's or authority's response to the overall policy statement?
ii) Are those statements which, in the context of policy, are more carefully focussed and targeted at a particular group eg young people?
iii) Are those statements which describe what it is your organisation or authority intends to do?

If then you glance again at the example given from Derbyshire you will see that it does respond to an overall policy, is targeted at a specific group and does describe what the authority intends to do.

The reader will know from experience that confusion often arises from lack of clarity in terminology so that aims, objectives, purpose, are often taken to mean the same thing. This is particularly so with aims and objectives.

Objectives

i) Are targeted statements describing the outcomes, from the user groups' point of view (as opposed to aims which describe what your organisation intends to do).
ii) Are desired end results.

If an aim of your organisation is 'to develop decision-making skills of young people' and your intention is to facilitate some training events to assist the achievement of such an aim it is necessary for your training event programme to describe objectives thus, for example:

From January 1988, the members council will decide on the content of future club programmes.

or

From next year, representatives of the organisation's membership will assist, with full voting rights, with the appointment of future staff.

When the policy, aims and objectives have been agreed and therefore 'owned' the next set of decisions relates to how these shall be achieved. By what methods shall the objectives be implemented?

Methods

Methods are a whole range of strategies which are intentionally designed to implement the aims and objectives; for example setting up mechanisms and relevant training whereby young people are actually involved in decision-making and not only appreciate the consequences of these decisions, but are responsible for their implementation.

A final part of this comprehensive action plan is that it should be evaluated. This term usually refers to significant aspects of the essential elements of policy, aims, objectives and method, and makes a judgement about their appropriateness and effectiveness. Examples of evaluation-type questions are as follows:

- Does the policy need changing?
- Were the aims relevant?
- To what extent were the objectives achieved?
- Were the methods appropriate to the achievement of the aims and objectives?
- Were the resources adequate?
- Is there need for specific staff development?

Figure 2.2 describes the interaction between the specific parts of this action plan:

If the aspects identified in figure 2.2 are not synchronised or are not even clearly articulated, good management is impossible and ineffective management is the only likely outcome.

Without clear statements of policy, aims and objectives which are the outcome of consultative processes, and thus 'owned', then an organisation or authority must necessarily be working on an ad hoc basis and lapse into arbitrariness. This can result in isolated styles of work and feelings of being unsupported.

However, once this work is done, and decisions made, you as an officer should be able to go about your task confident that there is clarity about the policy, which, without exception, should guide, limit and influence every activity.

Having established a policy through the process described above, all concerned must increasingly realise that this represents a contract between everyone involved. Many youth workers establish contracts with young people. It is part of the explicit, open and trusting relationship that should be a central characteristic of all our work. It is not acceptable for authorities or organisations, for example, to state their commitment to participation, to encourage

Figure 2.2 – Interaction between parts of a plan of action to implement policy

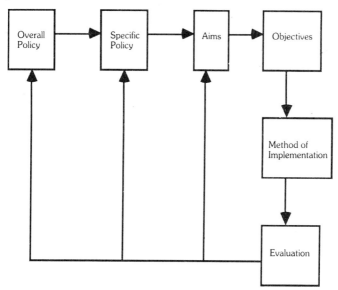

young people to develop their decision-making skills, and then exclude them from debate at crucial moments. My experience of young people is that they have the potential but are not often given the opportunity to learn by doing.

It is important therefore for your organisation or service to include everybody concerned in a careful and clear process designed to produce an agreed policy statement. Within a voluntary organisation this must include the executive officers, those who at the end of the day can say 'yes' or 'no'. Within a local education authority this must include councillors, who have the power to create policy and ensure that officers implement it. 'If I am directly affected by the decision, I should be involved in the decision making', is a statement with more than a grain of truth in it.

People are far more likely to show interest and motivation if they have been involved from the start in the shaping of the policy. The exclusion of individuals from decision-making in public affairs is much more likely to create a sense of the individual's powerlessness to influence policy so that at best she becomes apathetic and indifferent and at worst, cynical and anarchic.

Implementing the policy

In many ways discussion, debate, agreement about policy is the easy part. The crucial factor is whether or not the policy can be implemented. Are you actually implementing, in every facet of your work, the policy of your organisation or local authority? There are numerous factors which influence the situation.

Working with existing staff

If your organisation or authority carries out a review of its policy, in addition to being involved in its design the first people to consider when thinking about how the policy will be implemented are of course the existing staff.

Change is often painful. This may be for a number of reasons:

- Its direction is unacceptable or threatening.
- It takes place too quickly.
- It produces new demands which are not adequately resourced.
- It evokes a feeling of being de-skilled.
- It involves leaving behind relatively safe certainty and moving to relatively disturbing uncertainty.

In-service training programmes

Training is a central agent of change. Therefore within your organisation or authority it is extremely important that the trainers design training events which complement and facilitate the policy to be initiated and developed. This means that your trainers, as well as being familiar with policy and policy change, need to be in close touch with the managers and staff to ensure relevance.

Job descriptions

A third factor that influences the implementation of policy, must be the way we recruit new staff, and in particular the need for specific job descriptions.

It is no longer acceptable to appoint a person to a post because of proven ability in folk music, or a successful sporting career. The professional discipline that has emerged and certainly been encouraged by the structured approaches insisted upon by the system of accreditation of staff development policies by the Council for Education and Training in Youth and Community Work has been one factor in sharpening the professional practice of the youth services.

For example, if your agreed policy document states that within a personal and social education policy your organisation should have regard for the policy statement that follows, then all of these things should be stated in the information that accompanies the job description:

(a) securing the provision of appropriate information, advice and counselling;
(b) enabling and encouraging young people to set up and run their own activities and organisations;
(c) enabling and encouraging young people to be involved in the community;
(d) assisting young people to make the transition from school to work and meeting the needs of young people who are unemployed;
(e) meeting the needs of girls and young women;
(f) meeting the needs of young people who belong to minority ethnic communities;
(g) meeting the needs of young people who have special needs;
(h) promoting international visits and understanding.[2]

If, for example, you are wanting to appoint an experienced specialist to work with girls and young women, the job description should state specifically that the worker will be responsible for this aspect of work and the job specification would, in turn, indicate that the successful candidate should have, amongst other characteristics, 'experience in innovative work with girls and young women'. Conversely, if you are appointing someone to be responsible for the programme development of a number of clubs, or someone specifically to develop the partnership between voluntary organisations and local authorities, the job description and specification would indicate these aspects of skill and experience were essential requirements. But the watchword must be 'balance'. It is necessary to strike a note of caution in selection which prevents the appointment of a candidate who is strong (or professes to be strong) on the one particular policy or issue, but may be lacking in other key areas.

Finance

Little of this can happen without some financial resource. Within a sizeable voluntary organisation (as distinct from a local authority, see below), it is essential to understand from the start of your job as an officer just what budget exists, and what you have access to. The question needs to be asked whether or not existing resources and the regulations governing the way they are disbursed helps, hinders or can be changed to facilitate policy.

If there are other full or part-time paid staff in the organisation, who pays them and how are they paid? Who actions the monthly/weekly cheque? Are there, for example, any superannuation schemes? If so are they clearly administered?

There will normally be some kind of training budget. If so, how is it made up? Does all the money come from national headquarters? Or is it made up of proportions from unit subscription, headquarters allocation and a local authority grant? Does the organisation nationally or within your region have a development budget which can be used to fund new projects or help ailing units?

Does fund-raising form any part of your job or the organisation's work? This is an aspect of the job that requires clarity for all concerned. If fund-raising is part of your work, or that of the organisation, you need to know who is responsible for what.

If, for example, your organisation normally raises half of its annual budget you need to have an early grasp of how and when that money is raised. You would also be wise to build up a store of information on different ways of raising funds viz; business and industrial sponsorship and access to one of the many trust funds.

Whatever the size or number of budgets available to you, do you clearly understand how you can spend the funds? What systems/structures exist? Can any of it be spent at your discretion or does a committee have to approve everything?

As a youth officer of a local education authority there are similarities to what I have said so far. But the labels are different! If you are responsible, for example, for one district or area of a county authority you will need to clarify and understand the local rates of pay, the budgets and the appropriate administrative systems.

We have now considered four factors that influence the ability of your organisation to implement its policy viz:

i) Working with existing staff.
ii) In-service training programmes.
iii) Job descriptions within selection procedures for newly appointed staff.
iv) Financial resources.

Let us assume that you have worked as carefully as possible at those aspects of the job mentioned above. All being well you should now have sensitive, skilled and experienced staff recruited and trained to do the job.

Have you got the message so far? What I am saying is that it is a waste of time and effort if, prior to beginning work, the following are not in place:

- A clear agreed and relevant policy.
- Focussed aims.
- Specific objectives related to outcomes for user groups.
- Appropriate methods for achieving these objectives.
- A process for evaluating all the above.

The job is to implement the policy of your organisation or authority. Within the context of that policy you, as an officer, must begin to identify, within the area or organisation you work, what the needs are. How do we do that?

Identifying needs

The reader needs to be aware of some of the central characteristics often involved in need identification:

- Users are often in the best position to know what their needs are.
- Users sometimes require help in articulating those needs.
- Meeting needs is not a one-off event. People often require help to recognise that meeting some identified needs may trigger off awareness of other needs.

- Some needs can be met in isolation and others may require a great deal of complicated effort.
- People require help to understand that different strategies are related to satisfying different needs.
- Various needs, with varying degrees of complexity, involve different time scales.

It is sensible, if not essential, to ensure that the policy of your organisation or authority is reflected in the methods you adopt in identifying needs.

If, for example, your policies include a commitment to a consultative style of management, to encouraging participation at all levels, to creating opportunities for people to be involved in decision making, it would be hypocritical (and a missed opportunity) to identify needs in ways which are dictatorial, autocratic and non-consultative. I am quite sure the reader can identify individual youth officers who, for example, spend much of their time preparing, organising and directing cultural, sporting or training events almost to the exclusion of other staff and certainly young people. Though the event will probably be successful in terms of numbers of people attending or good organisation, very often opportunities are missed to enable other people to learn, grow and experience real responsibility. If such occasions are dominated by one person, who is learning? Whose needs are being met?

It is not unusual to observe a youth officer develop a project, organisation or area by working many hours, do all the thinking, planning, initiating, actioning, and repeat the exercise again and again over two or three years. In terms of people attending, it may be successful. It may be tremendously motivating for the officer in question. But who has learned anything new? Whose needs are being met? Were the voluntary staff asked to organise anything? Have the part-time staff, who do much of the face-to-face work, been asked for their ideas or been involved in the planning from the start? Have young people been asked to take some responsibility? Were their needs achieved?

If, when a worker or officer leaves for another job, most things continue to function and develop then it is usually an example of someone who had involved others, delegated responsibilities, empowered young people and asked all concerned to take the opportunity to learn something about themselves and develop their skills and experience. If, on the other hand, many of the weekly activities grind to a halt it may well be evidence of a situation where virtually everything was done by one person. This is a sign that the officer's needs were being met. She has been on a personal ego-trip called 'doing things for people'.

The point is this. Each officer involved in the youth and community business, should, in theory, be working on the basis that she and her staff will be out of work eventually, because the young and the not so young have learned to think for themselves, plan, organise and complete a project or programme. Charles Handy[3] describes this as internalisation:

> Internalisation ... is the form of commitment most desired by organisations. It is commitment that is self maintaining and independent of the original source of influence. But it is the hardest to obtain and takes the longest time. Internalisation means that the individual recipient of influence adopts the idea ... The change will be self maintaining to a high degree. But she (the individual), will also tend to believe the change was her idea and no one else's. This matters not at all in terms of the desired result but if you are the person exerting influence it is remarkably hard to let the recipient take all the credit for herself.

In reality of course, this rarely happens completely because communities and organisations are changing all the time, people move jobs and homes and take their experience and newly acquired skills with them.

It is much less time-consuming to do things yourself. Life can be much easier. But if you work in this way you are not working against the policy of the organisation or authority.

Having now established the base from which to operate, and emphasised that the policies of your organisation should be reflected in how you go about the job, let us imagine, for the purposes of this exercise, that you have been promoted to an officer post. Before priorities for action are identified or developed you must take a step-by-step approach which will both assist in identifying the needs and lead naturally to deciding which things get done first.

Step one: what exists now?

You are the county officer for a uniformed organisation. Though you may inherit a filing cabinet full of varied information, you need to check how many units actually exist and whether there has been or is likely to be any change in that number of units.

As a means of learning quickly and establishing some credibility in the field do this initial check thoroughly.

- Name of unit?
- Where do they meet? How do I get there?
- Is the unit financially sound?
- Who are the staff? How long have they been in post?
- A job description should exist, but if not, is there any record of the job they were asked to do when they were invested with the responsibility. Is there a clear 'contract'?

Having gathered as much information as possible make a personal visit, arranged in advance with the leaders involved.

- Arrive 15–20 minutes before the session is scheduled to start. This gives you not only an opportunity to check on the condition of the building, a chance to check whether the adults involved allow sufficient time for preparation, but also some time to talk to the young people attending. Try to establish good relationships with the leaders of the unit and do more listening than talking.
- What do you look out for? During your time there ascertain whether the building and facilities are safe. Someone needs to check if the electrics are sound, if that broken window is safer than it looks and is getting some attention, if the furniture and equipment is safe to use. Much of this can be done quietly without being officious in any way.

Is the building welcoming to young people? Is it warm? Though voluntary organisations very often meet in buildings owned by someone else, the quality of the meeting place should, nevertheless, be as attractive as possible. Through observation and discussion with young people and leaders find out as much as possible about the programme provision. This should tell you something about the amount of planning that goes on, and how relevant the weekly/annual programme is to the aims and philosophy of the organisation. Where possible talk to young people about their project/unit and its activities. Do they enjoy the provision? Are they involved in any way in making some decisions? Is it useful?

Do not rush your visit. Resist the temptation to get two or three visits in during one night or session. One carefully planned visit will save you much time later. Make a point of talking to all the adults either leading or helping in whatever capacity. Caretakers, for instance, can be a mine of information. Visits from county officers do not happen too often. You can use the occasion to register interest in the staff's work. This in itself is a way of valuing their contribution and winning their confidence and, hopefully, their commitment. Ask for their ideas and opinions and suggest they ring or write if they require some information or help.

This kind of thorough approach to each unit will take much of your early time with the organisation. The number of units will determine how long it takes, but will have established for you a detailed foundation of knowledge about what exists now.

- You will know the majority of staff.
- You will know the units and their whereabouts for yourself.
- You will have begun to assess the health of the organisation regarding policy, aims, philosophy, financial resources, staffing strengths and weaknesses.

   – You will have become known to a large group of people and hopefully have won their friendship, and established some trust.

What I have outlined so far in this first step has been aimed at the officer within a voluntary organisation. The same approach of course is also appropriate to an officer of a local education authority.

It is important for both to be knowledgeable about the specific responsibilities and tasks that members of staff have, and this includes their conditions of employment and what commitment, if any, they have within their contract, to training. This in turn assists the officer to determine at what level and in which context to talk about training.

As stated earlier, the job description should reflect the policies of the authority or organisation and is an essential document when, in time, you are reviewing the work of the unit or project. This will, of course, include the appraisal of the work being done by staff involved.

Step two: extending your information

Whether working for a voluntary organisation or local authority the next stage in assessing the needs is really going on at the same time as step one, but for descriptive purposes I will call it step two.

You need to extend your knowledge about the context, the community in which your units, projects or centres are placed. If for example you work in an area where a number of local coal mines or industries have closed down, that will have a major effect on the work of your unit.

Who are the major employers in the area? Where are the parents of the young people you are involved with likely to be working?

What is public transport like? Looking at a map can be very deceptive. It is very easy to assume that because of their geographical location local villages will automatically travel to the nearest town. Cultural tradition, places of work, school catchment areas and systems and direction of transport all have a bearing on which way people travel.

How much unemployment is there in the area? This and other information can be quickly gleaned from a conversation at the local job centre, or with a helpful careers officer, who will also give you an accurate resume of which Manpower Services Commission schemes are operating and how successful the take up is.

What is the commercial provision like? Many of our public houses, disco's and cafés are planned specifically to attract young people. It is important that a youth officer knows where these places are and how successful they are. In addition each locality has its gathering places for young people, particularly in summer. What happens in the local housing estates and shopping precincts?

It is important to know where the local schools and colleges of further education are and to establish contact with the principal and some of the staff.

Colleagues working in allied fields can also be very helpful, particularly the social services, probation and the local police. The findings of the Thompson Report[2] stated that the public did not understand or have an awareness of the youth service. That is as much our fault as anyone else's. The youth officer, together with relevant colleagues, has an obligation to heighten the awareness of the public to the services available and to the work going on. The most successful way of doing that is by involvement, which we shall discuss later.

At the start of this section on identifying needs I stressed the importance of ensuring that the policy of the authority or organisation should be reflected in the methods you adopt in trying to identify what the needs are. I hope you have noticed throughout this section, though without direct reference, how I am encouraging the officer to have a consultative style of management that should give staff and the local community a feeling of accessibility, involvement and an ability to participate.

Though the officer should be beginning to make some initial assessment of the needs of the local communities as well as the needs of your service or organisation, she has at this stage to remember:

- The officer has to apply the policy of her organisation/authority.
- The officer has to enable people to identify needs which the policy is intended to meet.
- There are many people's needs the officer has to identify and respond to vis-a-vis:

  - the needs of the organisation or authority
  - the needs of workers
  - the needs of user groups
  - the broad needs of the community.

- Figure 2.3 indicates the overlapping needs, and suggests the question: how does the officer respond to these inter-locking (and perhaps competing) needs?

The link between identifying needs and establishing priorities

Many an officer has come to grief as a result of precipitate action. 'This is what I think, and this is what I have decided we shall do'. With

Figure 2.3

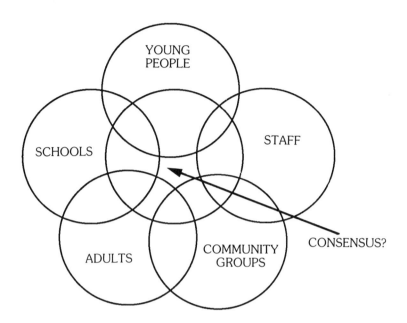

this kind of action, the response is often muted and many staff may appear to be less than enthusiastic. 'Why isn't it working?' asks the officer. Did those involved fully understand what was happening? Were they informed in advance? Were they involved in any way?

You may have come across that Chinese proverb about learning, beloved especially by trainers in adult education:

Tell me – I forget
Show me – I remember
Involve me – I understand

The link between identifying needs and establishing (causing people to adopt) priorities is the question of involvement. Which leads us to the third step.

Step three: development programme

As the officer in question you may be wondering about what to do next. You will also have some ideas of your own as a result of your initial visits, surveys and subsequent discussions with other staff and young people.

In seeking to get unit leaders, staff and young people to work with you on new ideas and approaches, consider the benefits of a development programme that grows out of staff conferences or meetings, rather than just your pen.

It is essential to determine the right size of meeting. It is often very difficult to feel involved in meetings of large numbers. Where this is inevitable it will be necessary to ensure that groups of eight or nine have the services of an experienced group tutor.

Though many assumptions are made about the aims of the organisation, it is very often sensible for your staff, young people and supporters of the organisation to refresh their minds together about what it is they are trying to do.

Having done that it is then that you introduce some of the suggestions you have received, including your own ideas, so that the group go on to discuss what they want to achieve (objectives), and how they feel the organisation should go about doing it (method).

If there is a suggestion that two units should close down, or that the policy of the organisation should alter radically, this is the opportunity for full explanation and discussion. This should ensure a measure of understanding, if not agreement.

Part of that debate of course will be resources. Can we action whatever we decide upon? Have we the facilities, the finance, the staff and support? In narrative form this may sound very simple and straightforward. Please, do not be deceived! These kind of processes may take you some time and a number of meetings. Eventually however, the discussion should lead to some general consensus where even if some individuals do not agree with the decision, because they have been involved, they should at least understand.

After all these needs have been openly discussed and the priorities agreed upon, it is time to ensure that the organisation understands who is doing what, which we can describe as defining the role. If an element of trust and understanding has by now developed, hopefully people will be willing to identify their strengths and weaknesses and agree who is going to do what (contract making).

Meetings, consultations, discussions also make it less easy for people to avoid commitment. Contracts (commitment, support) openly and publicly agreed in open forum are more likely to be honoured than those imposed or suggested privately or in letters/memos to individuals from officers.

Part of the process should lead naturally on to setting target dates for implementation and/or completion.

The last consideration of this developmental programme is the evaluation. There was a time when this was seen as something that was done at the completion of the programme or event. Much better to consider the benefits that accrue from agreeing an evaluation process that commences somewhere at the planning stage, and is undertaken by some group or individual separate from or external to the programme or event in question. The vital question to consider here is how will we know if the event/programme/course has succeeded?

Throughout, your staff, supporters and young people in the organisation have been involved in discussion which has looked at needs, decided what needed doing (possibly in priority order); who should do what and when. The most beneficial factor I feel is that good team work begins to emerge; a number of people have taken some responsibility; individuals have taken the opportunity to develop their skills and experience; there is ownership of the action and outcome.

There are a number of other factors to be considered in the third step which may be relevant to you as an officer of a voluntary organisation or local authority, depending on your particular situation.

As the officer concerned you will have made some initial assessments from your own point of view. You will have listened to the ideas and opinions of staff and young people as you were finding out what was going on in the area or organisation. What are you intending to do next? You would be most unwise to think that you can now, having done your homework, simply go ahead to implement your plans.

It is now a fact of life that youth and community work clearly operates within a political arena and it is this that makes up one of the additional factors I referred to. Elected members or councillors are members of organisation, district and county committees. They are elected by the local populace to represent their views and assist in the creation and implementation of policies to create better services for the people who live within the boundaries of the authority. These councillors, together with other local people from the community (a second factor) will usually make up the membership of a centre or district committee. They too have opinions and ideas about relevant policies to meet the needs of young people in their centre and/or community. They too must be listened to. They too must have an opportunity to outline their opinions and ideas. Committee members are asked to help in the management of projects, centres or areas. Understandably they will also have identified specific needs which may or may not coincide with the policies of the authority. If at this stage the youth officer implements her ideas or plans, without consulting local people, committees, or staff, it is likely that development will be a long time coming. The sort of consultation and sharing with local politicians outlined above may also be useful in persuading them to change policies which may be beginning to seem inappropriate either generally or locally.

It is necessary, remembering those policy characteristics of participation, involvement, developing decision making skills, to create a forum at which ideas and potential changes can be discussed.

Once again it will be wise to ensure a meeting or forum of not too many people. Much better to have two or more meetings than attempt one that is so large that effective learning and debate does not take place. Area staff can be involved in some planning sessions prior to the open forum taking place. A group of full and part-time staff can not only be of some help to the content and organisation, but can learn a great deal from this kind of involvement.

The local authority youth service is no different from the voluntary sector in that there has always been, and will always be, debate about what the policy ought to be. Consequently it is appropriate that at local forums, staff meetings, management committee meetings convened at this stage to consider needs and priorities, that groups be asked initially to consider the purpose of the service (aims), describe what they would like to achieve (objectives) and then decide on how the work is going to be done (method).

Let us assume for the moment that the policy, in general terms is about:

> developing a service with and for young people to aid their personal growth and development alongside enhancing an ability to work in groups and reinforcing a compassion for others.

Within the context of that policy, whether voluntary organisation or local authority, the local meetings or forums will then want to discuss whether existing provision is meeting the needs of young people. This may be a long and painful process involving much time and effort by all concerned. The young people will have some honest comments to make. The youth officer may be asked for her assessment of current work, indeed a group of people may be asked to assist the youth officer in the review of existing units or projects within the area.

These and many other factors will be considered in seeking to identify the needs of young people in an effort to assist their personal growth and development.

Any youth officer must learn that he or she is, or should be, an agent for constructive social change. At this stage in the debate she should remember some words from the Thompson Report[2] where the report stated that:

> for some young people the service may appear simply as a means of pleasurably extending their experience, to others it may be a real rescue service . . . it is important . . . to continue to fulfil both these purposes and not concentrate on one to the exclusion of the other . . .

So as the youth officer within the forum I have described, you may find on the one hand people saying that they are happy with what they have already, on the other a strong lobby of opinion advocating that three local youth clubs should close to enable a new counselling and advice centre to open for young people.

As an officer you have on one hand constraints of existing policies to conform to while on the other you may also be advocating that much of what exists should close down to enable new ideas to develop. The latter however may meet a wall of opposition from the local management committee members. What is the solution? Do you try and bulldoze your ideas through? Do you try and lobby the influential committee members or county councillors?

Though it is extremely hard work, and at times very difficult to organise, the decisions about which things take priority from amongst locally identified needs must be the outcome of openly discussed and sensible debate that has been furnished with all the facts, opinions and ideas and whose process has facilitated the involvement of young people and the participation of local groups and full and part-time staff in the planning, organisation and debate.

If we can be optimistic for a moment, and assume that priorities have been established, discussion will then move on to resources. If there is sufficient flexibility at local level it may be possible to staff and finance a development plan from within existing budgets. Alternatively it is possible that as a result of being involved, and the motivation that comes from that kind of process, the local people in the shape of a district, centre or project committee would be willing to submit an application to the authority or national organisation for a larger budget to facilitate new projects. Together with the officer, the group would probably go on to discuss who should do what, and agree target dates so that all concerned could begin to see the systematic approach developing what was advocated earlier. Part of the clarity about how the work was to be evaluated, and by whom. These kind of approaches should lead to real 'ownership' of the prioritised programme, the implementation and the outcomes.

Though much time, effort and patience is required of the officer and other staff if this style of management is adopted, it must also be stated that this approach makes many demands on the organisation or local authority, who need to accept that changes in administrative and financial systems may be necessary to accommodate this kind of work. It also brings us back full circle to the beginning of this chapter where I stressed the need for a clear and fully accepted policy by all those involved. In particular those ultimately responsible need to understand the implications from newly adopted policies. During the early years of community education in Derbyshire, Sir Jack Longland, the then Director of Education, stated that 'if we educate the community and ask them to participate, we must also expect them, at times, to march on the doors of county offices.' This may well be one consequence of a participative policy, designed to meet the specific needs of young people during their transition from childhood to adult status.

If we develop a youth service which is much more meaningful to young people we will then find ourselves adopting policies and a style of work that helps to identify the real issues which unite and divide a community. The wind of change comes through learning from the processes that emerge as a result of trying to identify and respond to local issues.

References

1. *Derbyshire Youth Service Policy Statement*, Derbyshire County Council.
2. The Thompson Report (1982), *Experience and participation, the Report of the Review Group on the Youth Service*, Command 8686, HMSO.
3. Handy, C. (1985), *Understanding Organisations*, Penguin.

3 Curriculum development

Penny Frost

'I leave it to my club leaders' the senior officer says thankfully, moving on quickly to the following chapter. But the design of club programmes, or the approach taken by workers on other kinds of projects, is the end product of the philosophy shaped by the senior officers and their youth committees, and should be valued as such.

Whilst collecting information for this chapter, I experienced this process in action. I had written to a number of youth workers in the Bedfordshire youth service, with whom I had worked previously as a trainer, to ask them how they approached the design of the programmes in their clubs. Several of those who responded sent me a paper called 'Social Education' which outlined the educational philosophy of their county youth committee, and the workers described how they used this statement as the basis for their own curriculum planning and evaluation. Although I shall refer to this in more detail later, I think it illustrates clearly how a youth committee can make a link between its own policy and its outworkings at club or project level. My example is taken from the statutory sector, but the link between beliefs and practice is also true for voluntary organisations, and the managers in each sector.

The term 'curriculum development' may stir up some recollections of lists of set books pinned up on classroom walls, or the thought of Old Chippy teaching Tudors and Stewarts to the Third Form because he always teaches Tudors and Stewarts to the Third Form ... but in this chapter (and widely, now, within the youth service) it has the sense of the design and evaluation and redesign of programmes of activity that youth officers and their workers wish to make available to their clients, to reflect the framework of beliefs held by those officers and workers about young people and their needs.

This chapter is structured in the following way:

1. Does youth work need a curriculum?
2. Learning in informal settings.
3. Planning and implementing programmes.
4. Evaluation and redesign.
5. Key points for managers about curriculum development.

1. Does youth work need a curriculum?

The current philosophy in youth services takes very seriously the function of youth work as a bridge between school and adulthood. Youth clubs are often described as a 'safe place' in which young people can begin to look at the changes in themselves and test out these changes in a number of situations, such as the personal relationships they make with their peers and the workers, and the responsibilities they take on within the club for particular activities. Youth workers may consciously or unconsciously steer away from any notion of the club as a 'place of learning', since they are sensitive to the needs of young people to have a place to escape from the heavy demands – or disappointing experience – of school.

However, they are working with young people at a time of great changes in their lives and are necessarily involved with supporting them as they experience those changes. Learning and change are inextricably mixed, and any worker involved in helping young people to reflect on their experiences inevitably will be part of their learning from it.

Although the term 'youth work' may still conjure up pictures of table tennis and club discos, it would be hard to maintain that the role of the youth service is purely recreational. For many years it has been recognised that youth work has an important function in young people's social development, and this has been borne out by the way in which most local authorities now place youth work within the compass of the education committee.

The 'Social Education' policy paper used by the Bedfordshire youth service, referred to previously, sets out skills required by young people making a successful transition from childhood to adulthood, and includes the management of personal relationships, the ability to be actively involved with community and political processes, understanding one's own limitations and personal resources, appreciation of the needs of others and the boundaries of personal freedom. Workers evaluate their club work against the points set out in this paper and find it a helpful reminder of their role in relation to their club members' personal development.

The Young Women's Christian Association (YWCA) is an example of one voluntary organisation which took curriculum development so strongly that it changed the whole direction of the organisation's work.

The YWCA traditionally provided hostels offering cheap accommodation to young women away from home, perhaps making their transition from school to work or to college. A little over a decade ago the management of the YWCA, recognising the importance of being alongside the young women experiencing transitions in their lives, and aware that the provision of hostels was tying up the resources of the organisation, decided to sell off a great many of the hostels. The sale of the properties released enough money to allow the YWCA to set up special projects to work with young women with particular needs. At that time the YWCA was concerned at the isolation and lack of assertiveness in the workplace of young women starting work as trainees or apprentices. They believed that women would not be able to develop their abilities fully within their chosen occupations without programmes of assertiveness training and structures to offer them support and break down their isolation, and so the energies and resources of the organisation were released to work to this end.

In the intervening years the employment situation for young people generally has changed dramatically, and more and more organisations from both the statutory and non-statutory sectors have set up projects to work with unemployed young people, to try to build up and maintain their self-esteem as well as helping them in a number of practical ways.

In each of these examples, the 'curriculum' – the approach to young people with particular needs – has grown out of the desire of certain organisations to target these young people in the first place.

2. Learning in informal settings

Preparing for a lifetime of learning

Senior officers in youth services typically find themselves preoccupied with policy and with the problems of resources: securing the budget, spending it and hanging on to the next year's. It is easy in these circumstances to become detached in time and space from the consumers of their services, the young people, and to lose sight of the educational intent of the activities which they are managing.

Sometimes national officers of organisations in the voluntary sector find themselves structurally very far removed from the end product: this is the experience of organisations such as the YMCA or the Youth Work Unit of the Church of England, who are servicing autonomous local units and have no direct managerial responsibility for them.

In viewing youth work as an educational activity, senior officers necessarily have a role in understanding the educational process involved, and enabling the process to take place effectively. Clearly, youth work is not educational in the same sense as the formal learning available in a school or college setting, and youth work does not follow a syllabus of learning drawn up by an external body geared to the setting and passing of exams. Outside the formal structures, the responsibility for shaping the curriculum passes to those taking part in the experience.

The implication of this for youth work as an educational activity is that the value of the learning experience for the young person is shifted from the end product – that is, the qualification obtained or the course completed – to the process of learning, where the experience itself can be a valuable contribution to the self-development of the individual. The value of self-direction in learning is that it offers a 'strategy' – an approach to learning – which enables any individual to tackle a whole range of areas as and when she or he feels the desire to do so. The opportunity to self-plan offers young people the experience of making their own free choices in how they handle their new situations as young adults. From this perspective, youth work emerges as a potential contribution to the life-long learning and development of young people.

Some key assumptions about learning

Over the last 15 years or so, considerable interest has developed in how people learn; what motivates them, what resources help them and how their learning should be organised. This has been particularly well documented in the fields of adult and management education. The main assumptions that have emerged have underlined the value of self-direction and mutual enquiry, and the need to use life-situations and experience as the richest resources for their learning[1]. I am sure that these assumptions about how adults learn have considerable relevance for the organisation of learning for young people. Indeed, they are entirely congruent with the beliefs about the experience and participation of young people in the youth service as put forward in the Thompson Report[2], which stresses the importance of young people's involvement in, for example, the planning of their club activities.

Supporting the learning

If the officer, having read to this point, is saying 'Yes, I agree with all of this; but it is a long way from where I am and how I spend my time', then it is important to remember the role of the officer in supporting the learning that is going on.

Here are examples of three ways in which the manager can offer support to the youth worker who is attempting to encourage learning among young people.

Firstly, by offering an overview of the work being undertaken in the club or on a special project such as unattached youth work. Learning in an informal setting does not have the same opportunities for being 'tested' by exams and assessment as are available to the more formal institutions, and the worker, who is very close to the event, can lose sight of what is being achieved. The manager's overview can be a very helpful insight to the worker in maintaining the shape and direction of the work, and help the worker to approach all experiences, both good and disappointing, as opportunities for her or his own learning. Self-evaluation on its own can easily turn into self-criticism and depression.

Secondly, the manager has more control over the resources than the worker, and sometimes workers need support for potentially risky ventures.

One part-time worker I spoke to told me about a fashion show organised by his young people as a substantial fund-raiser for the club. He described how the young people trailed around the shops borrowing expensive outfits from interested and supportive shop managers, and worked hard to learn how to present themselves on a cat-walk. He listed the learning experiences for those young people: writing letters and using the telephone to make the arrangements for the show; taking care of the costumes; learning to present themselves; handling the takings from the event – the list is a long one. He showed me a photograph of a smartly turned out young man looking bent on making it to the colour supplements, and recalled 'I never thought I'd see him in a suit. A few days before the event he got into a fight at the club and I tried to ban him. He said 'No, you can't ban me now. I've got to appear in the fashion show!' '.

In that instance, the role of the manager was not to help to identify what learning was taking place; the youth worker was very clear about that. But the worker needed to know that he had the trust of his officer to go ahead with a project that could have had heavy financial consequences.

Thirdly, the manager may need to support the worker who feels that no learning is taking place. For every club worker who has had success in encouraging young people to participate in the running of their club, there will be another who is baffled and frustrated by the apparent inability of young people to take charge of themselves, and the demands made by the young people on the worker. The stress for the worker in situations like this may be very great, and is linked in with a sense of failure, and the youth officer should be alert to the need to offer support to the worker confronted by 'non-risk-taking' young people.

It has already been noted that non-formal learning includes a process of mutual enquiry. Teachers involved in adult education may find that they and the students are mutually engaged in pursuing an exciting area of study. This experience may also be true for some youth workers with a burning interest in, say, sport or photography or pottery, which can be shared in the club. But for youth workers with a more general approach to their club work, the mutuality of the learning experience may be harder to perceive.

Because it is hard we should not ignore. Need to actively promote training opportunities with practical use.

The medium and the message

One further point about learning which I feel is important to bear in mind is the phrase which is very much the current parlance of educators and trainers: 'the medium is the message'. Its meaning is clear: whatever you are putting over to others must be made available in a style congruent with your message, or the impact of the message will be lessened or even cancelled out altogether. The often quoted example of splendid incongruence is that of the Religious Knowledge teacher, driven to the end of his tether by a particularly obtuse and difficult class, who has singled out one pupil to stand at the front and receive the message of the scripture: as the teacher's hand whips back and forth across the boy's face, he splutters 'Do you hear me, boy? God – is – love!' The need for congruence between medium and message for effective learning is an important aspect of planning programmes at any level.

3. Planning and implementing programmes

The senior officer is not normally involved in the planning and implementing of programmes or activities, except perhaps in cases where some delicacy of management may be required (some workers might say definitely *not* in those cases). However, as a manager of staff and resources, it is useful for the officer to be reminded of the processes involved in the thought-out design and delivery of youth work.

The key assumptions about learning mentioned earlier offer a clue about where to start; you begin with the motivations of the members. Probably the single greatest motivation for young people to join clubs or other organised youth activities is the opportunity to make personal relationships in an unthreatening environment which is acceptable to parents. Given this strong and fairly obvious motivation, leaders are likely to be looking for ways of building on such interest, and encouraging young people to be sensitive towards each other as they develop personal relationships, both with other members of their own sex and the opposite sex. Many club programmes are geared to the encouragement of healthy personal relationships among young people. This is what might be described and understood as mainstream youth work, and unites workers from the statutory and voluntary sectors as part of the foundation of their work.

An interesting development of this has been in the recent upsurge of anti-racist and anti-sexist youth work, which is the response of some youth workers to what they perceive as the intolerable behaviour displayed by particular groups of individuals towards other identifiable groups, such as boys' behaviour towards girls, or the behaviour of white young people to black. Programmes of anti-racist or anti-sexist work have been developed to try to challenge and change attitudes considered to be untenable within the club and within society. This development of youth work is particularly interesting because it moves beyond a desire to maintain the growth of the individual, into a desire to change individuals' value systems and therefore their behaviour. Youth work has been identified as an educational process, which inevitably implies change in attitude and behaviour. But the decision to work on changing values is a big one, and underlines again the importance of the senior officer ensuring that the link is strongly maintained between what is practised by the face-to-face workers, and what is the policy of the youth committee.

Anti-sexism and anti-racism work are good examples of programmes which may grow out of the observations and motivation of the workers themselves, or which can be initiated from above as a matter of policy. Either way, the youth workers will need support from their management, as an assurance that their efforts will not be disowned, or help in the form of training and resources as they tackle an area of work that might be unfamiliar or uncomfortable for them.

Work with girls

Alongside or as part of anti-sexist work, there has been the implementation of programmes of work specifically with girls, sometimes setting aside an evening a week as a 'girls' night', or organising a one-off 'girls' weekend'. This is in response to the common observation of the lack of use girls make of club facilities.

Boys encourage girls to be admiring audiences for their prowess at table football, pool, five-a-side, etc. The girls, once they have tired of being the admiring audiences and realising that they will wait all evening for their turn on the pool table, congregate in the ladies' loo and complain that there is nothing in the club for them.

In a booklet called 'Girls' Nights!'[3], the National Association of Youth Clubs posed itself the question 'why work separately with girls and young women?', and answered in the following way:

> Because teenage girls and young women generally have less self-confidence and lower expectations of themselves than boys, it is normally much harder for them to make their presence felt, and to participate fully in mixed sessions.

The booklet advocates a number of ways in which typical club activities, such as football or motorcycling, can be arranged in 'girls only' sessions until the girls have developed the competence to participate on a more equal basis with boys.

This is an example of how youth workers, by observing needs thrown up by the regular club curriculum, may attempt to effect change in the behaviour of the club members by changing or developing the curriculum in some way. As has been noted previously, education and change are inextricably linked. By attempting to change the behaviour of club members (in this example by helping the girls to develop self-confidence in competition with their male peers), the youth worker is encouraging the girls and, presumably, also the boys in the club, to rethink their value systems.

Shirley Jessop, a full-time worker in the Bedfordshire county youth service, ran a girls' weekend in Colchester. This is Shirley's account of the planning and experience of the weekend:

A particular event – girls' weekend in Colchester:

(i) How was it planned?

> A group of ten girls asked the female full-time worker if they could plan a weekend away together. The youth worker held two Saturday afternoon meetings with the girls (also one evening for parents) to enable the worker and girls to decide on the programme during the weekend and where they would like to visit.
> Colchester was chosen because Clacton was nearby and the girls wished to visit the coast. The trip included another female worker who was involved in all meetings. During the meetings the girls discussed what overnight accommodation was available with their financial restrictions and travelling costs. Youth hostelling was suggested by the youth worker and the girls consulted books from the local library and decided to stay at the Colchester hostel. The youth worker with the agreement of the girls prepared letters to the youth hostel and parental consent forms, and collected the money.

(ii) What was it intended to achieve?

> It was an opportunity for the girls to learn how to self programme.

They had to make decisions on the programme, which was difficult because of the wide range of interests. The girls were introduced to the value of using youth hostels and the travelling freedom they represent, especially abroad. It also proved to the girls that women can enjoy an educational and exciting weekend together without the presence of males.

(iii) What happened?

The weekend was a success in terms of everyone enjoying themselves. The programme was followed with some minor alterations. There was an unforeseen bonus: we came into contact with young people from France and Germany who were also staying at the youth hostel. The girls while in Colchester worked very hard at making the weekend a success. They were all responsive to discipline, readily helped with the chores and made friends with the workers at the hostel. When the group realised we might be back before the time given to their parents, we decided to make a detour and visit Cambridge. We had the opportunity to visit the colleges and play games in a park. Some friendships between the girls were strained by the end of the weekend but overall they all got on well.

(iv) How was it evaluated?

Each evening we, as a group, discussed the good and bad points of the day. We also made decisions on any changes to the next day's programme, if any. We also discussed how each member of the group had enjoyed it, and whether it was what we had planned in the initial meeting. Most of the girls asked for another similar weekend, but with the added activity of canoeing or climbing. The workers afterwards discussed the girls' behaviour and if they had achieved what we wanted them to achieve. We agreed they had, and had enjoyed working together.

Her closing comment about the weekend and its aftermath was:

The boys in the club felt excluded from this 'girls' only' outing, and were encouraged to organise something similar for themselves, but nothing concrete emerged from them.

I have included the detail of this account of planning the weekend, because it seems to me to be a good example of how every element of programme planning can contribute to the development of the young people concerned with it. Youth officers are a long way from the detailed design of events, and are likely to be in the situation of receiving reports on events which are deemed to have been 'successes' or 'failures' according to whether or not any fights broke out or ticket sales met costs incurred.

One implication of Shirley's account, for officers whose workers are involved in putting on activities and events specifically for girls, lies in her closing comment that 'the boys in the club felt excluded . . .

but nothing concrete emerged from them'. For some reason it appears that work undertaken to enhance the skills of one group within a larger assembly does not necessarily enrich the whole of that assembly. It is a point that officers might be interested in exploring with their workers when some specialist work is carried out, as it is an example of how workers are involved in making choices about their work according to their own value systems.

This point is worth bearing in mind for the officer whose brief includes some direct or indirect supervision of specialist youth work within the community, as well as club work. The questions for the officer might then be 'How does this project feed back into the community as a whole?', and 'Is it of relevance to the community beyond treating one section of it in isolation?'

Curriculum development in special projects

Youth work takes a number of forms across both the statutory and voluntary sectors. Many special projects have been set up to find ways of contacting and working with young people with particular needs. Some unattached youth work is set up in areas of high youth unemployment with the intention of working alongside young unemployed people, to support them as they look for work and encourage them as their energy and enthusiasm flags.

Other projects are set up in areas where a drug problem is suspected or known about among young people. Sometimes a particular social need is met by setting up an organisation specifically to deal with that need, such as the *Alone in London Service*, aimed at supporting young people who arrive in London without a job or accommodation arranged, and who might otherwise fall prey to unscrupulous pimps and the like. Larger organisations with an interest in such areas will often work alongside these small and single-issue projects. An example would be the presence of Salvation Army officers around the larger railway stations in London, looking out for young people on their own with nowhere to go, and working with the *Alone in London Service* in trying to persuade young people to return home, or at least to live in London safely in a hostel.

Projects such as these, set up to perform a particular task, do not necessarily have a sense of curriculum development. But projects where a worker is expecting to work for long periods with young people such as young unemployed, drug users or unmarried mothers need to be aware of their curriculum development. The worker will be aware of her or his attempts to encourage young people to reflect on their experiences, and to introduce ideas or activities which may encourage the young people to begin to develop a sense of their self-worth. It will be very slow work, without immediate or obvious rewards, and the worker will need the support of a managing committee or a senior officer to keep an overview of the development of both the project and the worker. Part of the overall development of the project may be to offer further training to the worker in areas where she or he would like to develop an expertise, such as counselling skills.

Assembling resources

Any youth worker engaged in developing and extending opportunities available to young people will need to assemble the back-up resources, and the common experience of youth workers is that materials and resources are in short supply.

However, one kind of resource is freely available in any youth work setting, and that is the combined experience of the workers and young people. In the key assumptions about learning, the use of experience was highlighted as the core methodology of informal learning.

As a manager of hard-pressed youth service resources, you may be warming to the value of building a curriculum around shared experience of members and workers, even if the educational philosophy of youth work leaves you cold.

In planning and implementing curriculum, most youth workers will expect to 'cut their coats according to the cloth'; in other words, to develop programmes which build on the resources, skills and opportunities available. These limitations in themselves can lead to some interesting and useful pieces of work.

Tina Troke and Marion Lowe, working together in a club in Bedfordshire, described to me how their club received a surprise 'face-lift' in just these circumstances:

> The club decor was incredibly shabby, neglected and unlooked-after – there was no sense of pride or of belonging to the club by members or even by staff. It was just a building.
>
> In the past the club had been decorated during a holiday period by the full-time staff and this received a lot of criticism, so it was felt that this time the members had to be fully involved.
>
> One of the part-time staff decided to decorate the committee room, as her project for part-time training, and very successfully got members involved either by actually carrying out the work or collecting posters and other materials needed. This project triggered off the idea (by the members) to decorate the rest of the building. The next step was for them to find out if the local authority would:
>
> (i) allow them to decorate the building;
> (ii) pass the colour scheme they had decided upon;
> (iii) arrange supply of the materials.

A letter was written from a group of members to the appropriate department, and they received a letter back and a visit from one of the county hall staff. They were allowed their colour scheme, told what materials they would need and where to collect them. The authority footed the bill.

Staff and some members then fetched the materials in the club minibus, and work commenced.

One group of about ten worked together very well, especially with one member of staff (the one that had been involved with the decorating of the committee room). Another member of staff criticized quite strongly about an 'elitist group of members', and felt that others were being excluded. Although this was partly true in terms of the numbers of members painting at any one time (as a result of supervision limitations), everyone (including other staff) had been invited and encouraged to be involved.

The person with whom we liaised at County Hall has since been in to look at the re-decoration, and is very impressed with it, and the club's 'new look' is something which a number of people have commented upon.

I asked Tina and Marion what had happened in the club about the 'elitist group' criticism. They said that it had all settled down amicably, but noted that since then, other pieces of work in the club had given rise to similar criticism – but directed at different groups. It is a common experience that work with small groups within a larger complex will give rise to feelings of envy and exclusion on the part of those who believe themselves to have been passed over. Managers who encourage their workers to undertake pieces of work with selected groups within groups should be aware of the potential for hostility that may result.

How planning decisions are made

The youth worker knows the value of encouraging young people to 'own' their own programme, and this requires them to have been involved as far as possible in the planning and organisation of their curriculum.

The worker whose fashion show I described earlier is a part-time worker in a club with no full-time worker, whose management committee is almost entirely young people drawn from the membership. Their commitment to, and pride in, their club is very high and he sometimes feels that because the club management is so dependent upon the young people, he avoids some of the problems experienced by full-time workers.

The International Youth Year in 1985 highlighted the importance of enabling young people to participate effectively in our society, and some youth services have made structural changes to encourage this in their own organisations.

Some time has now elapsed since the impetus for change provided by the Youth Year, and managers of youth services might take this opportunity to review what change has taken place in their own organisations, and how far young people are able to take responsibility for the planning and management of the youth work with which they are involved.

4. Evaluation and redesign

I began this chapter by describing curriculum development as an on-going process of design, evaluation and redesign. This model is based on the model of experiential learning put forward by Kolb[4], in which the learner reflects on her or his own experience and applies the conclusions drawn from this reflection to inform the next stage of activity. That in turn becomes the learner's next experience on which to reflect, and the cycle continues. This model of learning is congruent with the value placed on young people's experience in the key assumptions about learning described earlier in this chapter, and offers a helpful approach to curriculum development in youth work.

In the terms of this model, evaluation of each programme experienced by young people and youth workers is a critical element of the cycle, as it should be providing the feedback to the worker necessary for the effective redesign and development of the curriculum being offered.

There are two further reasons for carrying out evaluation of both on-going programmes and special events. One is that it gives back information about how far these activities are contributing to the overall aims of the youth service. The other is that evaluation can highlight the effectiveness of training techniques used, regardless of the purpose of any individual event.

Youth workers often have rather haphazard structures for evaluation. They would expect to be making regular reports to their senior officer, and perhaps produce an annual report and projection of their work for their youth committee, and this provides some opportunity for review and revamping. They may exchange some hurried comments with co-workers or voluntary helpers whilst the doors and windows are locked up at the end of a session. But it may be difficult for them to find both the time and the appropriate structure to undertake the more searching review and evaluation of their programme which makes it possible to note developing trends, or the particular set of values which they may be projecting by the work they are carrying out.

Probationers have this opportunity when they work with non-managerial supervisors, and I am interested to note that several of the innovative pieces of work described to me were started by workers undergoing their training (although not necessarily working with supervisors). It is, perhaps, easier to be innovative when you are paying attention to your own development in a job. In contrast, full-time workers can experience a great deal of isolation in their jobs – it is not always possible to get together with one's colleagues, and workers are not necessarily enough at ease with their line management to seek out opportunities to review their own work.

It is very difficult for workers who have an emotional investment in an event or set of activities to carry out evaluation by themselves, although they can be part of an evaluation process. This suggests the need for someone with less emotional commitment being involved in regular evaluation, who may be the area officer or equivalent, provided that sufficient trust exists in the management structure for it to be workable. These are points which should be taken very seriously by managers in youth services, if they are committed to encouraging growth and development within the youth service curriculum.

5. Key points for managers about curriculum development

(a) You are managing an educational enterprise.
(b) Youth work is generally taken to be in the area of social development and education. Does your youth service have a policy which sets out what its youth work should achieve?
(c) Learning follows from the experience of a particular event and reflection on it. Learning is enhanced when a young person is encouraged to draw upon her or his own experience, to be as self-directing as circumstances allow. How far is the learning process enhanced in your youth work setting?
(d) Effective education may result in changes to the value systems of those participating in it – workers as well as members. How far are you concerned with the changes being brought about and able to link these changes back to the policy of your organisation?
(e) Educational activities need to be evaluated regularly if they are to develop. Do you set the criteria for the evaluation of the programme and special events? How are these criteria transmitted to the workers who will be carrying out the evaluation?
(f) Youth workers have too much investment in their work to be

able to evaluate it effectively on their own. Yet evaluation is a key element in curriculum development. How can you devise methods to help your youth workers to carry out effective evaluation?

(g) Go easy! Please don't take on (b) to (f) all at once, or you will make your youth workers very worried people!

References

1. Knowles, M (1973), *The Adult Learner: A Neglected Species*, 2nd Edition, Gulf Publishing Co, Houston, Texas.
2. The Thompson Report (1982), *Experience and Participation, the Report of the Review Group on the Youth Service*, Command 8686, HMSO.
3. Bowlby, A (1984), *Girls' Night! Report on the Fulham Girls' Project*, National Association of Youth Clubs.
4. Kolb, D A, Rubin I M, McIntyre J M (Eds), (1974), *Organisation Psychology*, Prentice-Hall Inc, New Jersey.

4 Accountable for change

Alan Twelvetrees

I was asked to write this chapter partly because I have some
experience of working with the kinds of organisations, or parts of
them, with which youth officers relate. However, my experience of
these organisations has mainly been from the perspective of a
community worker. Moreover, I have never worked as a youth
officer. Therefore, in order to gather appropriate material, I
interviewed a number of youth officers. I was interested to discover
that in some respects youth work has become 'youth needs' oriented
during the last few years, and that some of the insights I brought as a
community worker (now a community work teacher) struck a chord
with the youth officers I was interviewing; the growing emphasis on
youth participation, for example.

I have tried faithfully to represent the practical wisdom of the
youth officers I interviewed, who all impressed me with their
commitment and ability. However, I have put the data gained from
them through the filter of my own perspective, and so take full
responsibility myself for the relevance or lack of relevance of this
chapter to the work of youth officers today.

The purpose of youth work

The aim of this chapter is both to examine the organisational
structures with which youth officers relate, especially those to which
they are accountable, and also to suggest how they can most
effectively work with and within those structures.

However, the context in which this chapter is set is one where
major changes are taking place within the youth service and indeed

have been for some time. The youth officers of the nineties will probably be working in the following ways. While they will continue to administer club-based services they will also be developing approaches to do with enabling youth workers to identify the needs of young people and to develop policies and curricula which meet those needs in systematic ways. In a sense, the youth officer now seems to be becoming a development worker, change agent perhaps, who encourages and supports the attempts of youth workers to identify the needs of young people (or to get them to identify their own), and secures financial, human or organisational resources so that those needs can be better met.

This work is inherently dynamic, since identifying and meeting needs in a changing situation is a never-ending process. It requires certain skills from the youth officer, which initial training does not always provide, and those of the social entrepreneur in particular. It requires the ability to create new organisational structures, youth councils and local youth work consultative committees for example, and to ensure effective youth participation on managing bodies or even on local authority committees. Some key words are 'participation', 'political education' and 'accountability'. However, it is accountability with which this chapter is largely concerned.

In many respects there are more similarities than differences in the work of statutory and non-statutory youth officers. It is convenient for the purposes of this chapter, however, to consider their roles separately. It also needs to be borne in mind that, while the term youth officer is used throughout, the functions undertaken by youth officers are carried out by staff with a wide variety of designations. It is hoped that what follows will be relevant for all those with some overall responsibility for youth service administration and development at district, county and, in some respects, regional levels.

Accountability for the statutory youth officer

Upward accountability

If the task of a youth officer is to ensure that youth workers meet objectives which are predicted by, let us say, a further education sub-committee – to run an activity-based youth club for so many hours a week for example – then that youth officer's task is a relatively simple managerial one. In that situation she is in turn managed by, for example, a deputy further education officer. Their joint concerns will be largely to do with deploying staff and the financial and administrative business of providing a service. There may be a youth officers' group which deals with information sharing and administrative matters but which has limited scope because the goals of the service are clear and relatively static. The youth officer will provide reports to her line manager about activities run, number of young people attending clubs etc, and thus the formal accountability process will take place.

The traditional bureaucratic system of line management described above is to a large degree suitable where a member of staff has to achieve clear objectives specified from above, and it is to some extent appropriate to the work of the youth officer who is concerned with managing club-based workers.

However, questions need to be asked about the suitability of traditional bureaucratic forms of organisation to the management of officers whose task is to respond to the changing needs of young people. Senior managers who are concerned primarily with administering a service may not be prepared to take risks, may want to see a concrete output in terms of competitions organised, for example, and can sometimes be reluctant to spend time throwing ideas around. The youth officer who is trying to innovate may have difficulty persuading this kind of line manager to consider new approaches, and will probably have to justify any new proposal in great detail by, for example, showing evidence that the particular scheme advocated is already operating well elsewhere. In this kind of situation the youth officer may have to spend an inordinate amount of time negotiating with and seeking to persuade her line manager. In the last resort she may have to seek ways of bypassing or outmanoeuvering her, but this course of action is likely to backfire and is not recommended.

The key to many changes is personal relationships. If a worker can establish a good relationship with her superior – and this may need working at – then that superior may be more prepared to listen to new proposals, particularly if these are couched in terms which coincide with the objectives or the value systems of her superior. To do that, the worker has to spend time understanding how her superior ticks, which may not be easy if she is a bit remote. People in senior positions who are resistant to change are often afraid of something – of failure perhaps – and the youth officer needs to understand why her superior has the attitudes she has if she is to influence her. Such people are often under pressure themselves, from council committees and politicians for example, and know that if a mistake is made, the youth service budget may suffer. Thus their conservatism may be a consequence of the pressure they are under, rather than a personal characteristic.

A useful resource here can be the peers of the youth officer, if there are any, and senior youth workers. It is not usually difficult to find a few like minds who can work together to get new policies adopted. Agency change within an organisation which is resistant to change, and, indeed in any other, requires low to middle level staff to organise collectively as a starting point. Once the staff are meeting together then strategic and tactical decisions have to be taken about whether to go direct to a resisting manager or to adopt a different approach.

Changing a conservative agency from below is usually a very slow process. Often, field staff make one attempt which has not been carefully thought through, fail, and do not try again. They then continue to plough their own furrow, concealing what they can from their superior, and not influencing policy. One alternative approach is to try to select small achievable objectives first, and develop a plan as to how they can be achieved. This sometimes involves doing nothing, or at least waiting for certain senior people to retire. An experienced youth officer once related how she had spent 18 months carefully introducing the idea of a different fee structure for room bookings, which was then implemented. If she had gone any faster she would never have achieved it. See Resnick[1] for further ideas about changing one's agency from below.

In a youth service which has adopted a more dynamic need meeting approach within an overall policy framework accountability of the youth officer and tasks to do with development are interrelated. In one local authority the senior county officer meets regularly with her deputy and the six area officers together with representatives from the staffing section of the further education department. These meetings were established to monitor and review developments and arose from the formulation of a policy for the youth service. In this authority, while major policy changes have to be decided by the further education sub-committee such changes are sometimes initiated by this group. The group members are encouraged by the county officer to contribute to the agenda and initiate policy discussions. Thus an atmosphere has been created where an individual youth officer can say 'I tried to get this particular project established. It did not work. I'm not quite sure why. Can we discuss it?' As there is a policy framework in the authority in question, there is usually a rationale behind action taken by the youth officer.

Not all actions have the intended effects, but the group can then examine what went wrong and, in an atmosphere of trust, learn from the mistakes. This particular authority has just set up an innovative basic adult education project, and the youth officer who established it told me that she could not have obtained local authority agreement to go ahead if this policy review group did not exist.

However, making this kind of structure work requires a particular kind of commitment from the youth officer to play a full part in the meetings. This involves contributing to the agenda and consulting with other relevant people not attending the meeting for whom a specific agenda item might have particular relevance. A youth officer who was involved in this group emphasised the importance of building relationships at all levels, upwards, downwards and laterally in order to inform himself and inform others so that they too were involved, at least in a small way, in the policy making and review process. It is interesting to note, however, that this group was 'thrown together' for many hours in order to design the youth policy in the first place. The members got to know each other well and obviously found they could work together, which, sadly, does not always happen. Working effectively in such a group requires a number of skills, inter-agency liaison skills, listening skills, organisational skills, and a preparation to be open about our work.

There seems to be two main problems with this kind of approach. First, there are occasions when youth officers want to take up an issue, such as regrading, where their interests might well be different from those of the more senior staff with whom they have collegiate relationships. It is difficult to change roles so that one minute the youth officer is discussing an issue with a senior colleague more or less on an equal basis, and the next is raising a grievance. My own view is that the collaborative policy planning process has to be separated off in time and perhaps place from the more formal aspects of employee/employer relations. A related point is that this open system cannot work if the various group members cannot participate in an open way.

The second problem is rather different. A dynamic youth officer working with a range of others to develop and implement policy is likely to be creating an enormous amount of work for herself. Unless she rations her time she is likely to suffer from 'burnout', namely a state of anxiety and lethargy resulting from overwork. Moreover, unless she is clear about her own objectives she may be blown off course by conflicting pressures from people representing other interests, all of whom wish to get her to do what they want.

Elected representatives also have a part to play. It is the policy of the group mentioned above to include elected members in policy-making at a very local level rather than purely at the formal sub-committee level. For example, they are involved in interviewing applicants for part and full time youth work posts.

In addition, some youth officers have a good deal to do with councillors on a day to day basis. One youth officer said (and I paraphrase) 'Some local authority officers are afraid of councillors finding out what they are doing and tend to keep elected members in the dark. But I believe in trying to educate councillors that the policies which I am trying to implement are for the good of people. If you are successful with this open approach it helps you to work in a relaxed manner'.

However, relationships with councillors can be problematic. As they are elected on a ward basis the allocation of resources to their ward can be a very sensitive issue. Since most youth officers cover more than one ward an officer can be caught in the crossfire between feuding councillors. To say the least, a sensitive awareness of the local political system is essential for the youth officer.

Lateral accountability

Relations with other departments and other professionals can be more problematic, however. Official county policy will have been approved by the council. But it also has to be negotiated in detail with (rather than imposed on) headmasters, social services departments, colleges of further education and so on, all of whom have somewhat different priorities. When dealing with lateral relationships it is important to look at what kind of meetings need to be held, and with whom, to make sure that problems do not arise, or that they are nipped in the bud. A case in point would be deciding how to stop school caretakers preventing a policy about dual use of school premises being effectively implemented. If the youth officer does not plan ahead in this kind of way she is likely to be involved only in crisis meetings.

A youth officer is also likely to be a member of other groups, committees, working parties and project planning teams, from an individual youth club management committee to a home-school liaison group and a crime prevention advisory panel. Involvement in such groups requires the kinds of skills mentioned earlier, particularly the skill of understanding the interests of other participants. But it requires, in addition, that the youth officer thinks clearly about her own objectives. For example, is she there to be a full member of the group, or is her job to advise about what the youth service can offer in that particular respect? Again, clarity about her own role within a clear policy framework will prevent the youth officer taking on too much. There are also implications here for good quality guidance, supervision and consultancy to be available to the youth officer as she goes about these tasks.

Downward accountability

The main role of the youth officer should be managerial, but in the best sense of the word. Today her job is, within an agreed policy

framework, to negotiate with her field staff ways in which they can
identify needs and develop curricula which meet those needs. She
then has to ensure that the resources (staff, money, training, plant)
are provided so that the identified objectives are reached. Another
role is to provide advice for non-statutory youth workers and
projects, (dealt with later in this chapter). However, the youth policy-
making and implementation process also requires a form of
downward accountability, in addition to informing or consulting.

Some authorities now have local consultative groups for youth
and related work, involving youth workers, local councillors,
representatives from community organisations, community centre
user groups and so on. Such consultative groups meet perhaps four
times a year to discuss youth needs at a more local level. It is also
common practice in some places for youth leaders to submit reports
to them. These groups give youth service personnel a chance to
explain what they are doing to a slightly wider audience and to root
their work in a wider perception of need. They are one means for
ensuring that issues of concern are fed into the system. When they
work well they can be an effective means of public relations, and in
some places elected representatives value them highly. But, again,
there has to be a commitment to make them work. Sound
preparation is needed, and, in some cases, contact with the
members between meetings in order to keep up their interest, to help
them think about the questions to be discussed and to work out what
to put on the agenda. The youth officer may also be involved in
booking rooms, circulating minutes and so on, all of which are
apparently simple tasks but which need care if they are to be carried
out well. Managing meetings and 'servicing' groups of people running
their own meetings all require skills which are not common currency
and which are often carried out less effectively than they could be.
See *Working on a Committee*[2] for some practical guidance in this
respect.

A further dimension of downward accountability is liaison with
community groups. Community groups are increasingly involved in
welfare provision, and professional workers such as youth officers
now need to be able to relate to them. However, those who have not
had much to do with community groups are often surprised by what
goes on in them. They can be remarkably effective or ineffective.
They can be either welcoming or hostile towards professionals. They
usually survive with great difficulty and keep going only because one
or two stalwarts ensure that they stay in existence. They may be torn
apart by hostilities between members. Most of all, they are
autonomous and they guard this autonomy jealously. If a youth
officer is planning to undertake a piece of work with a community
group she needs to think carefully about it, discuss it with her

supervisor, try to arrive at an agreement with the members about what she is there for, and, preferably, read about work with community groups as well. See Twelvetrees[3] and Henderson and Thomas[4] for guidance on work with community groups.

Accountability for the youth officer in a non-statutory organisation

As is mentioned above, the general role of the voluntary organisation youth officer (subsequently referred to as the *youth officer*) has certain similarities with that of her statutory counterpart, who is concerned with policy development and implementation. It also should be noted that some youth officers in the voluntary sector operate at national level, while their counterparts in the statutory sector do not. However, it is not my concern here to explore the unique aspects of the work of voluntary sector youth officers operating at national level.

In the context of moving towards issue-based youth work from, say, recreational youth work, the officer is concerned with generating the resources and providing back-up on the ground to voluntary sector workers, so that the people doing the face to face work have the appropriate conceptual tools as well as the practical resources to do the job. The youth officer's role in this process is often to develop organisational structures suitable for issue-based work. But the voluntary organisation youth officer is usually accountable to a committee, and it is this to which we now turn.

Upward accountability

In some committees the purposes of the organisation may not have been clearly thought through, or it may not have adapted to changed circumstances. Consequently, the attitudes and skills of the committee members may well have become irrelevant to the requirements of the organisation. Like youth centre workers, youth officers often get the committees they deserve and the staff may well have to work hard to recruit effective members.

Committees may also become full of 'worthy people' who are there primarily because of their status, rather than because they have specific skills or knowledge. If there is a preponderance of such people the committee can become remote from the young people or the youth workers who are concerned with the actual performance of the organisation at field level.

Local authority representation on the committees of voluntary sector youth service organisations also needs to be considered carefully. What, for example, are the roles of local authority representatives on such committees? How and to whom do they report? What, if anything, is being communicated to important colleagues, senior managers, and elected members? Quite often these matters have not been thought through. The example which illustrates this problem is that on one such committee, with county-wide responsibilities, there were four local authority officer representatives, each of whom had an area brief, in an authority with seven area teams. Yet, there was no officer representation from county level.

In this situation it was necessary for the youth officer to identify others who, in her view, were both willing and able to make an appropriate contribution to the committee, and to find ways of getting them to join it. There are many different ways of achieving this and it is impossible to prescribe how it should be done. Moreover, when working to change her committee the youth officer has to think carefully about how to time her interventions and whether, for example, she herself should raise delicate matters with the chair, or whether she should get somebody else to do it. Another method is to encourage outside organisations to seek representation on the committee or to arrange for constitutional changes to be proposed. However she does it, the youth officer needs to ensure that new individuals are identified who can make an appropriate contribution. Sometimes it is necessary for somebody to persuade the traditional leadership to retire. In other situations it may be more appropriate to wait until a new opportunity presents itself, when a vacancy arises on the committee, for instance.

The youth officer also has a responsibility to help her management committee manage. Most of the committee members will be involved in other activities and will be giving up their free time to be on the committee. They may or may not know much about youth work. Moreover, they may not understand the role of a voluntary management committee, which is to set policy, ensure the resources are there for the work to be carried out, manage the chief officer, hire senior staff, deal with grievances and so on.

In the USA it is widely accepted that voluntary management committees need training and consultancy, though the idea is only slowly being accepted in the UK. If the committee members accept that the organisation is failing in some respects to meet objectives, they may be prepared to engage a consultant to help them examine performance in the light of changing needs. This can be a very good way of helping them perform their functions more effectively. Moreover, it can also lead to the resignation of those members who are not prepared to adapt their approach, thus leaving places for other people with more appropriate skills to offer. See series by Feek[5] for further information on how to manage community-based organisations.

It is usually easy for a youth officer to manipulate or bypass a weak management committee so that the youth officer becomes a law unto herself. But that is a recipe for perpetuating a weak committee, which is in nobody's interest. The youth officer does need a good chair, who can make her reflect, and a good committee whose members can discuss policy in an informed way, particularly in times of crisis. Therefore the officer needs to work at creating an organisational culture within her management committee, similar to that which was obtained in the local authority youth officer's policy group, mentioned above. It should be remembered, however, that the *voluntary* sector youth officer is one person working to a management group (through a chairperson) while the *statutory* youth officer is a member of a group of peers working in effect to a senior manager.

The voluntary youth officer is also in a rather strange and isolated position. She may well span different levels of the corresponding local authority hierarchy. In organisational terms she is the peer of a local authority chief officer, in salary and overall status a peer of middle or lower managers, but in much of her day to day work a peer of full time youth workers. The different levels of organisational space occupied by the chief officer of a voluntary organisation can sometimes give relatively easy access to all levels of the local authority hierarchy, including chief officers and fieldworkers and, in certain respects, more direct access to elected members. On the other hand she is also in a rather exposed position with no real peer support. Therefore, she must work hard to create a 'critical support' structure around her. (This is important with all posts where the worker is not part of a team.) One such youth officer consciously sought out other youth officers with a similar outlook to her own, met regularly with them, and eventually got one of them to join her management committee. Another arranged to have managerial supervision from his chairperson, but, recognising that the chairperson was not an expert in youth work, arranged for consultancy from a retired youth officer.

A voluntary youth officer who is concerned to see that the needs of young people are met is often led into an entrepreneurial way of working, trying to make the best out of limited resources, creating new resources from almost nothing. Thus, she will be working with a range of statutory and voluntary personnel at a variety of levels, trying to get them to work together. She may well be in contact with housing, social services, police and other departments, to try to ensure that they develop policies geared towards the needs of young people. She will also be aiming to educate councillors and act as an advocate towards them on behalf of young people and their needs. To do this she may have to involve those councillors in some way in youth work policy-making, or approach those who are already involved, such as any who are on her own management committee. It is well worth spending time with sympathetic or relatively sympathetic councillors in order to help them understand the service which they are offering.

There are, however, other ways of influencing politicians. One youth officer organised a conference on youth work policy for politicians, officials, full- and part-time workers and young people, thus allowing the politicians to learn from the clientèle. Another involved young people and part-time youth workers on her management committee, for the same purpose. Another managed to set up a joint member officer group with the council, on the basis of the Thompson Report[6].

In progressive organisations, voluntary and statutory, a culture is emerging which concerns participation, linking between different departments and authorities, the involvement of the workforce, managers, councillors and to some extent consumers in collaborative problem solving, the careful identification of objectives, together with a self-critical concern to evaluate the effectiveness of services. The youth officer, statutory or voluntary, is one of the key people involved in this process, which involves liaising with a variety of individuals and organisations and participating in a number of different working groups.

This new way of working has its stresses. To a large extent, the voluntary youth officer is dependent upon goodwill and resources from the local authority. One youth officer said 'It is almost impossible to involve those who do not believe in partnership'. It took this worker five years to involve one team of local authority workers in the training of senior members, which she had initiated. This worker also admitted that she was sometimes seen as an empire builder.

It is clear that a voluntary youth sector officer has to ensure that at least a small group on her management committee shares her ideas, so that she can run the organisation with them. This is particularly important if at the same time the management committee is to become more open and democratic. For instance, one worker ensured that the constitution was revised so that youth leaders and part-timers could be represented, but found that their ideas were often very 'traditional'. However, since the leadership rested in effect in the hands of a progressive group, the more traditionally oriented field level staff were educated by and carried with the leadership. This process was to do with recognising the contribution people at all levels could make and was thus about valuing them. It was also to do with open rather than closed organisation.

Lateral acccountability

Youth services in Britain are beginning to take on a youth policy, need-meeting approach, and committed youth officers can probably now do a good deal to influence the youth service as such. However, it seems to be more difficult to involve other agencies such as police, social services, housing and the formal education system in youth policy-making. One youth officer was involved at county level in discussions with these departments and reported rather limited progress during a five year period.

The attitudes towards young people of staff in formal education and of the police, for example, are often poles apart from those of youth workers. The key to policy changes in other departments at county level may lie partly in work with other professionals at local level, either through the kinds of consultative groups mentioned earlier or through work with the management committees of individual youth projects, which sometimes involve headteachers, socil and health workers, community activists and councillors. Either way, the skills of inter-agency liaison, covered in Chapter seven, are vital.

Downward accountability

A voluntary sector youth officer is not usually accountable 'downwards', that is to the people with whom she works, in any formal sense. But we have already seen how she may seek to ensure that those with whom she is working are represented on her management committee. She may even arrange an election among the constituencies served by her organisation whereby they themselves choose who should represent them. This kind of representation enhances communication and understanding between the officer and the voluntary youth organisations with which she works. But this downward 'accountability' works the other way too. Typically, a youth officer will sit on the management committees of several non-statutory youth projects, or at least advise them. In that process, if she is doing her job well she will come to understand the issues which are bothering people at field level, and may alter her own priorities accordingly. One voluntary sector youth officer was on the management committees of six clubs, centres or projects, all of which were facing different problems. One such group, composed of community activists, needed advice on the responsibilities of a management committee. In another there was conflict between the staff. Yet another was managed by a board of directors which owed much of the approach it took to management in industry. In another there were severe financial problems. In those groups the youth officer played a variety of roles, management consultant, a worker support role, trouble shooter, information giver, advocate for young people, to name but a few.

A voluntary agency youth officer is likely to have to manage her own agency, secure and manage funds, supervise a secretary and a caretaker and perhaps a small number of other professional staff, ensure the office and any other plant, such as a minibus, is in working order and so on. This function of managing her own agency, which a statutory youth officer does not usually undertake, should stand the officer in good stead when her task is to provide organisational advice to others. The skills required are again the skills of the community worker in so far as they involve advising people how to run their own projects. But they also include the skills of project planning, agency design and management and they should include the skills of evaluation. As is inferred above, these skills cannot be learned overnight. They require an ability to stand back and analyse what is going on, to understand how all the people with whom one is working see the world, to allow them to identify their own needs, put them in contact with others who have already overcome a particular problem, find out where they can obtain information, help them clarify their objectives and work out how to achieve them.

I wonder who provides the youth officer of today with these skills?

References

1. Resnick, H (1975), The Professional – Pro-active Decision Making in the Organisation, *Social Work Today* 6(15): 462–7.
2. Clarke, S C (1984), *Working on a Committee*, Community Projects Foundation.
3. Twelvetrees, A (1982), *Community Work*, Macmillan.
4. Henderson, P, Thomas, D N (1980), *Skills in Neighbourhood Work*, Allen and Unwin.
5. Feek, W (1982), *Management committees practising community control*; (1982), *Who Takes the Strain?*; (1982), *The Way We Work;* (1983), *Steps in Time*; (1984), *Value Judgements: Evaluating Community Based Agencies*, National Youth Bureau.
6. The Thompson Report (1982), *Experience and Participation, the Report of the Review Group on the Youth Service*, Command 8686, HMSO.

Postscript: I wish particularly to thank David Matthews and Jim Rooney, without whose help this chapter could not have been written.

5 The manager's role in training and staff development

Malcolm Payne

If, like me, you believe that we are all capable of growing and learning – widening our experience, broadening our understanding, increasing our skills – then perhaps there is no need to justify staff development. For it is no more than the means by which those things can occur.

And if, like me, you believe that the youth service, like the individual staff on whom it is built, is capable of continual growth and development, then again, there will be no need to justify staff development. For in my view, it is the principal means by which such growth will occur.

And finally if, like me, you believe that youth and community work has a duty to ensure that it maximises the potential of its staff by ensuring that their performance is continually improved, then staff development as a means to that end will form an essential feature of any management strategy. Indeed, youth and community work cannot be effectively delivered without it.

Whether staff development processes are formalised, becoming part of an organisation's policy, or whether they are merely part of custom and practice (unwritten policy?), the roles that individual members of an organisation play are critical if those around them are to learn and develop. The purpose of this chapter is to examine the staff development role of one of these: the manager.

By its very nature, youth and community work has many managers. Indeed, so complex is the picture that it almost defies description. But for the purposes of this chapter, a loose definition of who the manager is will be most helpful. By a manager, I mean *anyone who has responsibility for the work of others*. Central to this role is the youth officer, but full-time workers, part-time workers, volunteers – perhaps even lay members of a management committee, are often managers of others.

Two fundamental assumptions underpin the chapter: first, that the manager plays a key role in any staff development activity; and second, that sole responsibility for staff development cannot rest with any one individual in an organisation – the training or staff development officer for example. I hope that the reasons for both of these assumptions will become clear as the chapter proceeds.

What is staff development?

Since 1980, and the publication of INSTEP's *Guidelines to a Staff Development Policy*[1], widespread acceptance (at least within the statutory sector of the service) has been gained for a definition:

> An agreed framework and procedure for the enhancement and enrichment of each individual member of staff, through personal development, through job development and through organisation development.

Whilst this has proved to be an acceptable definition of a staff development policy, and the *Guidelines* themselves an outline of the content, we must look beyond it for an understanding of staff development practice. For ultimately staff development depends upon what people do, not on what policies say.

As individual organisations have sought to make this definition usable, they have adapted and amended it, but its central features have remained – particularly its focus on the person, the job and the organisation.

Outside of youth and community work, similar and parallel thinking has been taking place. Alex Main[2] for example traces a variety of staff development models in education, and argues for one which recognises the human being as learner, as needing guidance and support towards the exercise of choice. Staff need not to be imposed upon, not left lonely and exposed: their institutions and professional organisations need to share responsibility and choice with them.

Later in the chapter I shall be suggesting ways in which I believe that the content of staff development – the vehicles for its delivery – can now be expanded in the light of experience, but for now it is worth briefly reviewing what INSTEP believes that content to be. In summary, this is concerned with: Matching the right person with the right job (recruitment and selection); providing a systematic introduction to a newly appointed person (induction and probation); ensuring that there exists a clear and up-to-date statement of the scope and purpose of each job (job descriptions); the provision of ongoing support and direction (supervision); the evaluation of progress and identification of needs (appraisal); the provision of learning and development activities (training).

Such a brief summary will inevitably have masked a number of nuances; the *Guidelines* themselves provide a much more comprehensive explanation and are, in my view, essential reading for all managers. It is clear however that INSTEP sees staff development as concerned with much more than the provision of training. Indeed, it is fundamental to this approach that no amount of training is likely to compensate, for example for a mistaken appointment, or the problems caused by poor job definition. Put another way, training is seen as largely ineffective unless the other elements of staff development are present. It is seen as one important element in a package whose delivery is designed to contribute to the development of the individual – both as a person and within the job-within-the-organisation.

It is also apparent that it is no easy task to detect where staff development begins and management ends. None of the features listed above could be guaranteed to occur unless someone ensures that they do (a management task); many of them involve the manager in their delivery and are, of course, concerned with how jobs are done (a management concern). Conversely, the package itself is no guarantee that person, staff and organisation development will occur. Each of its features, while containing the potential for development, can be defined and practised in a way which contributes not to learning and growth, but to a confining and bureaucratic control.

This is a familiar tension between the needs of the individual and the needs of the organisation, and its parallel, the social education-social control spectrum lies at the heart of much people-work. It may have become a truism to suggest it, but it is nonetheless inescapable that our own ideologies and values, as well as those of the organisation in which we work – and the society in which that organisation operates – will affect the ways in which we work and manage. Staff development is as much a part of that value system, reflecting, reinforcing and challenging dominant ideologies. The alternative is to believe that management – and staff development – are purely technical tasks, akin to maintaining and adjusting machinery.

The person, the job and the organisation

Each of us, as staff members in an organisation, carries a triple identity: as person; as person-in-the-job, and as person-in-the-job-in-the-organisation. Whether that organisation is a large statutory or voluntary hierarchy, a small co-operative agency or any variation in between, these three dimensions provide boundaries for our actions.

As person, I bring with me my own unique set of strengths and weaknesses; skills, knowledge, experience, attitudes, values and ideologies. None of these is fixed once and for all; even experience, whilst not by definition able to be undone, can be added to, reflected upon and reinterpreted. Each of us is capable of growth and development given the appropriate opportunities. Similarly, each of us is capable of entrenchment and atrophy; unable to use our skills to advantage, immobilized. Each of us is capable of choice and may have a view of how best the job is to be done.

Every job is also unique. Whilst it may share with other jobs – both within and outside the organisation – many similar features, the requirements for each will be different; involving relationships with different people; facing different environmental factors (social, political and economic); and requiring different emphases. Many jobs across youth and community work involve a set of core tasks: face-to-face work with young people, finance and administration, the management of staff. Each of these requires of the post-holder a high level of interpretation and discretion, particularly about method. Beyond the core tasks, there is normally the potential for a range of initiatives open to an even greater degree of choice. Such flexibility contains both advantages and disadvantages: it can provide the opportunity for experiment and innovation, using particular strengths and enthusiasms; it can also deflect attention away from the main purposes of the job, even to the point where purpose becomes confused or undermined.

Organisations also vary widely; as do their component parts. Even within a single profession – youth and community work – radical differences in aims and purpose can be detected between organisations. And within organisations, both subtle and marked differences can be identified in how those aims and purposes are interpreted by different parts: units, teams, areas, regions and so on. How organisational aims and purposes are articulated also varies. In some, detailed and lengthy policy documents exist, though even amongst these there will be wide differences in how such policy has come about – the extent of staff participation, for example. In other organisations little is written down. Policy is merely the accumulation of decisions made over the years, what might be called custom and practice.

At either extreme – where there is no clearly articulated policy and little sense of priorities, or where policy is so rigid that little room is left for professional discretion – staff development may be difficult to achieve. At one end, relative success or failure (progress towards identified goals) may be difficult to measure. At the other, rigid and inflexible controls may hamper development and innovation.

Organisation culture

The culture of an organisation describes a number of these features: how and where decisions are made and control exerted; how policy is made and the extent of freedom of action of the individual within it; the patterns of information flow; its structures.

Charles Handy[3] has classified organisation culture into four different types:

- The *power culture*, in which authority tends to reside at the centre, with little bureaucratic control, and where decisions are taken (often very quickly) by a few key individuals;
- The *role culture*, in which clear procedures exist through set hierarchies, roles are clearly defined and little innovation demanded;
- The *task culture*, which tends to be job or project orientated, influence widely dispersed, highly adaptive, responsive and flexible;
- The *person culture*, in which individuals are all-important (structures existing only to serve them) and little overt control is exerted over their actions.

Organisation culture can be used to describe and analyse whole organisations – a local authority, a national voluntary organisation – or a part, such as the youth service within a local authority; or a subpart – a district, a team or a unit. Most managers operate both within a culture, (that of the larger organisation), as well as having the opportunity to influence or even create one (within that part of the organisation for which they are responsible). It is worth noting that Handy's thesis is not that one culture is intrinsically better than another, but that some cultures are better fitted to some tasks than others. For example, where rapid innovation around changing client needs is required, then a task culture can be effective in bringing together teams of experts to tackle new problems. But as increasing stability or long term development become necessary, a role culture will tend to emerge even though staff may prefer to work in other ways.

To the manager as agent of staff development, organisational culture is an important consideration. It will tend to affect how job descriptions are used, for example, or how appraisal is operated – if at all. It will be an important determinant (amongst others) of management-staff relationships, and therefore of the perceived purpose of supervision and how accountability is expressed.

The culture of an organisation and the preferences of its staff can be determined in a reasonably scientific way using the instrument designed for this purpose by Roger Harrison[4]. It can be a useful way of opening up discussion about the nature of the organisation in which people find themselves, and beginning the process of critical debate about how well fitted it is to the tasks in hand. It is one way of describing the relationship between person, job and organisation.

These three foci of staff development interrelate with one another in dynamic tension. Each gives rise to expectations; each creates needs to be met. Conflict will necessarily arise at certain times, but many of those needs are shared: to have a sense of purpose and direction; to receive feedback about progress; to build upon strengths and develop from weaknesses. Conflict and tension are not unhealthy. They can provide the 'potential difference' across which learning can flow.

BOX 5.1

A local authority youth service I worked with had been operating a staff development policy for a number of years. Part of my task was to help it evaluate how successful this policy had been.

In the course of discussions it became clear that some staff were unhappy with the supervision they were receiving, whilst others were quite satisfied. Was it simply that some officers were better supervisors than others?

We began to discuss the nature and purpose of supervision: the needs of the organisation, its officers and staff. What was meant by support? What information did officers need? What was meant by accountability? How was performance judged? By whom? How do people learn best?

At times, the debate generated a great deal of anger as different perceptions emerged. Doubts were expressed as to whether the debate was doing more harm than good.

Some of the conflict could be resolved by negotiation: recording supervision sessions was necessary, but passing the recordings up the line served no useful purpose and the practice was discarded. Others remained: youth officer A still maintained that dropping into a club once a month for a chat counted as supervision, but reluctantly agreed to try a different style.

So what had changed? On the surface, very little, except that the organisation had begun to discuss how it was working, some of its values and methods. People in different positions had begun to recognise their own needs and those of others, and identify ways of meeting them.

Some potential for change and development had been created.

Much of the rest of this chapter is concerned with harnessing the energy arising from that potential difference by looking at some of the opportunities open to managers to create staff development. Before going further however, it is worth considering three particular features common to youth and community work organisations.

Voluntary management, managing volunteers and the role of the adviser

It is common in youth and community work for the management of staff to be directly in the hands of a voluntary group, a management committee for example. In some cases, the management function may be divided between a professional line-manager (part of the organisation hierarchy) and a voluntary group. This is frequently a source of some difficulty unless clear lines of responsibility and accountability are established and roles properly negotiated.

Where management is solely in the hands of a voluntary group, however, there is a real risk that opportunities for staff development will be absent. Anthony Lawton[5] has suggested that, just as management committees try to recruit financial expertise to their membership, so they should try to recruit management and staff development expertise also. If this were the case, then much of what is said in this chapter would apply to such people. They would be nominated by the group to act as managers on their behalf, by for example offering regular management supervision.

As for the management of voluntary staff, it may be thought that this is in principle different from the management of paid staff. It is not customary for example to recruit or select them in the same way, or to provide job descriptions. It is as if the service has developed a peculiar ambivalence towards its voluntary workers. On the one hand, representing as they do the vast proportion of the total workforce, we clearly value and depend upon their services. On the other, they are frequently expected merely to fit in, with little attention paid to how they are selected, to ensuring that the tasks they are to undertake are made clear. Perhaps we feel that, because they are giving their time freely, we must not over-formalise the relationship nor make our demands too heavy.

And yet, in many organisations, volunteers also form the uppermost tier of management, with the paid officer seen as the servant of its voluntary executive.

This ambivalence is particularly noticeable where paid and voluntary staff work alongside each other. Roles frequently overlap and little distinction is made between those who receive payment and those who do not. Some careful attention in this area, whilst not removing the tensions, will go some way towards removing some of the frustrations experienced by voluntary staff. The support and training of voluntary (and paid part-time) staff has been given a great deal more attention since the publication of *Starting from Strengths*, but even here it has stopped short of considering some of the other features of staff development in any detail. Whether for example, clearer recruitment and selection procedures or the use of job descriptions might not bring greater clarity to the role of the voluntary worker. How highly are we valuing youth and community work – and the contribution of the volunteer – if selection is laissez-faire and there is no clear agreement about roles and tasks? It is a complex question, but comparison with organisations outside the youth service is revealing. The National Marriage Guidance Council, for example, has rigorous selection procedures which appear to bring high status to the job of the voluntary counsellor. Within the youth service, many youth counselling and advice services also select their voluntary staff with great care. Far from making it difficult to recruit volunteers, the increased status which this brings about may actually make the job of the volunteer more attractive. Certainly, within the field of youth counselling, where selection methods are more exacting, tasks clearly defined and regular supervision an accepted feature of the job, volunteers are not deterred from coming forward.

BOX 5.2

A youth club recently asked me to assist them in a team-building exercise. The club had a full-time leader, five paid part-time staff and a dozen volunteers.

Part of the exercise involved asking each person what they thought the others did in the club – and what they expected them to do. The underlying tensions soon became apparent.

Through a series of staff meetings, work in small groups and sessions with the club leader, the process of clarifying roles began. Whilst the term 'job description' was never mentioned, each of the voluntary and paid staff began to define and negotiate their role and how it fitted with that of others.

In the process, people were able to say what they liked and did not like doing; what they were good at (and what they felt others were good at); what they would like to be doing – and what they needed others to do.

This apparently simple exercise allowed the club to begin to discuss what it was really there for, what resources its staff brought to it, and their different responsibilities. The process of staff and organisation development had begun to occur.

A third feature common to youth organisations is the position of advisory staff. Such posts are common in both the statutory and voluntary sectors, with many officers having advisory rather than direct management responsibility for staff. The extent to which these officers see themselves as managers, having a direct responsibility for staff development, will clearly vary from post to post. Two things can be said, however. First, that it is to be hoped that advisers will see it as a primary task to ensure that clear management and staff development arrangements exist for all staff for whom they have a responsibility. And second, that there is great overlap between the management and advisory roles: managers frequently act as advisers or consultants to staff; advisers frequently have a staff development function. Much of what is written in this chapter will also apply to advisers.

Management styles and responsibilities

Returning to my central theme, I have defined for the purposes of this chapter, a manager to be anyone who has a responsibility for the work of others. This section discusses the nature of that responsibility, and its implications for staff development.

How managers interpret their responsibility will vary from one organisation to another, and from one manager to another. It is a defining feature of organisation culture. In youth and community work, as in many other contexts, it would be a fallacy to pretend that the manager has direct and continuous access to the work of others. For some, this will be a source of frustration and disappointment. Their (or their organisation's) need to control the work of staff may lead them to identify ways to bridge this apparent gap in the span of control. Supervision and appraisal for example are seen primarily as fulfilling the function of accountability.

For others the discretion and freedom inherent within dispersed organisations is a source of strength and challenge. Here perhaps staff are seen, if not as autonomous, at least as inherently trustworthy – as professionals in their own right. This is the spectrum which Douglas McGregor[6] has called 'Theory X' and 'Theory Y'. At either end managers will define staff accountability differently, and, it is claimed, behave differently. This is not the place to summarise the literature on management styles and leadership, merely to note that as managers we all have a preferred or dominant style, and that, like the culture of the organisation in which we operate, our style will have a marked effect upon the way that we operate as developers of staff. The 'best fit' approach[7] argues that there are three principal features which need to be taken into account in understanding leadership: *leader, subordinate* (sic) and *task*. In any situation the best fit between the style of the leader, the needs and expectations of staff, and the nature of the task, will prove most effective. A fourth factor, the *environment* (including the culture of the organisation) must also be taken into account.

As managers, we must operate at different times with different people whose levels of ability, motivation and performance will vary. Not only will there be differences between people, but in the same person at different times, and in the face of different tasks and organisational expectations. This may require of the manager an ability to shift gear, to range across a number of styles at various times. Our dominant style – our tendency to respond in set patterns – will limit our choices as to which is the most effective style to adopt at any one time. Best fit theory suggests however that changing style alone may not in the long term be the best course of action. Handy suggests that more long term benefits are likely from re-designing the task, or developing the work-group or team, both of which are elements of staff development.

The purposes of staff development

From a discussion of the person, the job and the organisation; from some understanding of organisation culture and management styles; and from the starting point of a belief in growth and improvement, some purposes for staff development begin to emerge:

- to assist individuals and organisations to relate more effectively to human and social needs;
- to provide the conditions in which the motivation and commitment of staff to meeting the aims of the organisation is maintained;
- to provide for the continuing development of individuals, groups, and teams to meet new and emerging needs;
- to assist in harmonising individual, group and organisational goals and aspirations.

Put alongside the INSTEP definition of staff development quoted earlier, such a set of purposes, if accepted, begins to answer the question which that definition poses: why 'enhance and enrich'? Put simply, the answer to that question is that the tasks of youth and community work cannot be accomplished effectively without staff development. It is a necessity, not a luxury. It is an essential part of the task of management.

The management task

It was suggested at the beginning of the chapter that the boundaries between management and staff development are difficult to identify.

One reason for this I have suggested is that staff development is one of the tasks of management. Another reason is that staff development is not always a discrete activity, separate from any other task. Any organisational activity can, to a greater or lesser extent, provide a vehicle for the development of staff. Planning, for example, whilst not in itself a staff development activity, clearly has implications for the development of individuals and groups. A planning process which fails to involve staff will not only fail to take their needs into account, but will run the risk of undermining their motivation and sense of ownership of the plans. Furthermore, the plans themselves may fail to take account of their personal strengths, resources and aspirations. The same is true of other management tasks.

A simple management model is often illustrated as in Figure 5.1 below.

For me, several observations can be drawn, even from such a simple model. First, that the management task is dynamic. Needs do not remain the same, nor indeed are met once and for all; management is based upon ongoing development and improvement. Part of that process must involve us in discussion about the nature of the need and how meeting it might fit with other objectives.

Second, with an eye to staff development, it is clear that opportunities for staff development occur at each stage of the cycle (just as those with an eye to the participation of young people will also note that opportunities for their involvement are also present at each stage).

Figure 5.1

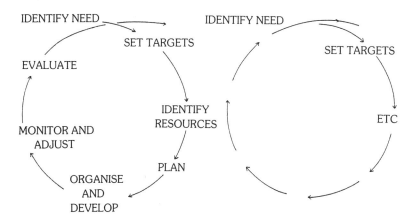

Third, not only does the model reveal the opportunities for staff development present within the management process, but applied to staff for whom the manager is responsible, it represents the process of staff development itself. For the manager-as-staff-developer, the starting point will be to identify need, to set targets, to identify resources ... and so on, as with any other management activity.

This seems to me to be key to an understanding of staff development, for it identifies it as a legitimate management task, alongside others within an organisation, with its own needs for knowledge, skills and experience from the manager.

Allan D. Pepper puts it like this:

> Every manager is a teacher. He teaches in a number of different ways; he teaches distinctly different things; and he teaches different sorts of people. Compared to a university lecturer or a school teacher his teaching responsibility is likely to be much more complex. Yet it is not customary to think of managers as teachers, and very many do not think of themselves as such. But if the effective teaching capability of management is poor, then so will be its training and development work.[8]

Forgiving him the overtly sexist assumption that all managers are men, and understanding teaching in its widest sense – as the enabling of learning and development – his message is clear. The next part of this chapter will apply the simple management model in Figure 5.1 to the process of staff development and suggest various ways that the manager can bring about learning and development – for individuals, groups and the organisation as a whole.

Identifying needs

Whenever identifying needs is discussed – particularly training needs – the conversation will fairly quickly turn to the model being used. Is it a deficiency model – one which describes learning needs as arising through some shortfall in performance? Or is it a potentiality model – one based on the assumption that we are all capable of further development?

The reality is that both models are needed: some needs will arise because individuals or groups are not performing effectively; others because things have changed and there is room for development. In either case, however, the difficulty may be not in identifying that a need exists, but analysing what that need really is.

But this is not to assume that it is only the manager who identifies needs. We are all involved in that, and when it comes to performance, it is often the performer him or herself who is the best judge. As someone said to me recently when discussing staff development: 'We must all design our own climbing frame'.

So the manager's task may be to encourage and contribute to

critical self-assessment and to create the climate in which needs are made conscious and can be acted upon. It is rarely the case that people are unaware of their own needs, though they may need the right conversation, at the right time, for those needs to be fully recognised and articulated. Of course, the wrong conversation, at whatever time, can send us all scurrying for cover, especially if we are operating in a climate in which it is considered questionable to have needs at all and where need and failure have become synonymous.

Each focus of staff development will give rise to needs at the level of person, job and organisation. Putting motivation theory to one side (for example Maslow[9], Herzberg[10]) it is nonetheless necessary to identify some of the factors which give rise to needs at each of the three levels.

Personal development

All of us wish to feel that we are growing and learning towards some (perhaps vaguely identified) life and career goals: aspirations both personal and professional. This does not necessarily imply 'upward mobility', though this will be important to many; it may indeed be the reverse (or perhaps 'outward mobility'?) for those approaching retirement or seeking a better balance between their personal and working lives.

Certainly, the caring manager (and organisation) will ensure that needs for personal development, career development and personal growth, are identified and, if possible, met. And in youth and community work, where such a high premium is placed upon personal skills, it is rarely the case that the organisation will not benefit in some way from such development. Frequently however, organisations will devise a sliding scale of financial support available to staff for development activities, which depends upon some notional calculation of the extent to which the organisation is likely to benefit.

Most supervision and appraisal schemes will have, as one of their goals, the identification of personal development needs, but again, it must not be assumed that the manager is always the right person to identify them. Outside expertise, in the form of career or personal counselling, consultancy or advice, will be appropriate at times.

Job development

Needs for the development of skills, knowledge and attitudes arising from job tasks will arise from the normal processes of change. Sometimes old skills need to be updated or refreshed, sometimes new learning is required to meet new challenges. In the past ten years youth and community work has required major job development activity as workers have faced the challenges posed by, for example, unemployment and homelessness, and by a growing awareness of the effects on young people of race, gender and disability. This has not only required new thinking, but also the application of old skills to new situations.

It is also clear that job development needs will arise from asking the question 'Could this person do the job more effectively?' Mager and Pipe[11] avoid the problem of deficiency v potentiality by describing *performance discrepancy*: the difference between *actual* and *desired* performance. They point out that many performance needs we identify are actually only symptoms, and that the evidence upon which judgements are made needs careful analysis if the real need is to be uncovered, and only then can decisions be made about possible solutions. Critical Incident Analysis (see for example Heron[12]) has developed an approach to identifying and analysing needs which can be used with groups and individuals. The major advantage is that by avoiding considering performance in a general way, across a whole range of tasks (and thereby risking superficiality), attention is focussed on one important area of work in depth. Many have found this to be a more satisfactory approach to supervision and appraisal than the traditional lengthy agenda.

Organisation development

Organisation development needs arise from considering how the organisation itself, or a part of it, is performing. Here, attention is focused on aims, purposes and methods, rather than individual performance. The frame of reference – a unit, a team, a district – will to some extent be determined by the extent of the manager's responsibility, but the model below is a useful tool in identifying and analysing development needs at a variety of organisational levels.

Each section of Figure 5.2 gives rise to questions which have implications for organisation development, as well as for personal and job development. Using the diagram as a basis, an agenda for discussion of a range of organisational issues can be built up as a springboard for action. This approach is described in detail in a recent publication from the National Youth Bureau[13].

One important feature of needs analysis is raised by this approach. Here, individual performance is seen, not in isolation, but as one factor in a more complex picture. It is not assumed that 'peformance discrepancy' is necessarily a result of inability or lack of individual skill (and therefore to be resolved by training). Needs which appear to arise from the performance of the individual frequently have their cause elsewhere: lack of job clarity, conflicting purposes or inappropriate use of resources. The diagram re-emphasises this, suggesting an alternative approach.

Figure 5.2

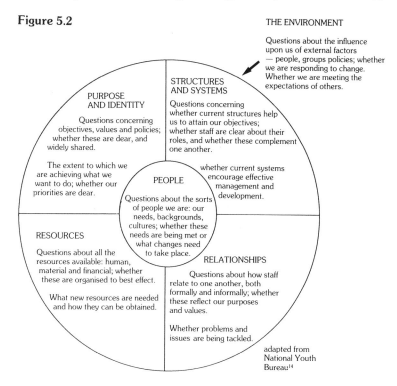

THE ENVIRONMENT

Questions about the influence upon us of external factors — people, groups policies; whether we are responding to change. Whether we are meeting the expectations of others.

PURPOSE AND IDENTITY

Questions concerning objectives, values and policies; whether these are dear, and widely shared.

The extent to which we are achieving what we want to do; whether our priorities are dear.

STRUCTURES AND SYSTEMS

Questions concerning whether current structures help us to attain our objectives; whether staff are clear about their roles, and whether these complement one another.

whether current systems encourage effective management and development.

PEOPLE

Questions about the sorts of people we are: our needs, backgrounds, cultures; whether these needs are being met or what changes need to take place.

RESOURCES

Questions about all the resources available: human, material and financial; whether these are organised to best effect.

What new resources are needed and how they can be obtained.

RELATIONSHIPS

Questions about how staff relate to one another, both formally and informally; whether these reflect our purposes and values.

Whether problems and issues are being tackled.

adapted from National Youth Bureau[14]

Two final points about needs analysis. First, that unless highly objective methods are used for measuring performance against agreed criteria (uncommon in youth and community work), then different perceptions of performance are inevitable. I may believe that my performance is satisfactory because it achieved result X; you may believe my performance unsatisfactory because it achieved result X. This is a disagreement not about performance, but about purpose, or desired outcome. The consequence is that the real need is not to improve my performance, but to resolve our disagreement.

BOX 5.3

A youth officer asked me to help him to identify the appropriate training course for a member of staff who had been in post for just over a year.

The full-time leader was, he felt, highly disorganised, had no clear club programme and seemed to be having difficulty with her staff. How could she be helped to improve?

The leader's view was somewhat different: certainly, she

*acknowledged that the staff group was not a happy one, but she felt that
her and her officer's views of what constituted a good programme were
very different. She felt it was important to challenge some of the norms of
the club she had inherited: she wanted the club's members to take more
responsibility and to give young women the confidence to articulate their
needs.*

*How did her staff feel about this? They were used to a more structured
approach she said, and were finding it difficult to adjust to her style. She
did not feel she was being well supported by her area officer to develop a
strategy to meet the needs she perceived.*

*From a very complex situation, we agreed upon some ways forward,
recognising that our perceptions of the 'problem' had changed as we had
begun to discuss it. The leader wished to be clearer about what she was
trying to achieve; she needed to talk with her staff about this and to
clarify her expectations of them and them of her. The area officer had
begun to accept that different styles and approaches were legitimate; he
would need to find a way, through supervision, to negotiate goals and
methods with the leader; to begin to support her in clarifying and
achieving these. Both recognised that some external help - consultant
supervision - would assist the leader in her task, while the area officer
needed to find out more about approaches to work with girls and young
women if he was to begin to support this aspect of her work.*

A training course would not have helped.

Second, that identifying need is very different from identifying
solutions. It is very tempting at times to confuse the two, or even to
try to identify needs upon which to hang some favourite (or
convenient) solution. Training is often used in this way.

Setting targets

Although for ease of illustration, setting targets in Figure 5.1 comes
before identifying resources and planning, in reality the three cannot
be kept entirely separate. There is little point in setting targets which
cannot be reached, or for which resources are unlikely to become
available.

That said, however, three key points need to be made in relation to
targets for staff development. First, that any target needs to be
agreed by whoever it might affect. This will certainly include both the
manager and the member of staff, but will often require others to be
consulted as well. If I am to spend time in the coming year developing
my counselling skills, this may affect my work with other colleagues,
with my management committee and so on. Their agreement may
need to be sought if I am to be successful. Second, targets must be
achievable. If I do not have the personal resources - the capacity for
some particular new learning, for example - then a target for
development in that area is a waste of time. If it is a critical area, then
a redefinition of the task, or a reallocation of other tasks, may be

more effective. Third, targets for staff development should, like others, be open to measurement. I should be able to demonstrate that I have for instance increased my skills or knowledge by changes in practice. If necessary, learning objectives and criteria which will provide evidence of development can be agreed.

It goes without saying that targets for performance improvement can arise from any of the four quadrants of Figure 5.2, as well as at the level of the individual job.

Identifying resources

Traditionally, the task of identifying – and providing – learning and development resources has been seen as the role of the training officer (or someone with a similar responsibility). More recently, we have come to understand that role in wider terms (see for example 'Core Competencies of the Trainer'[15]). Whilst the role still requires the training officer to provide and manage learning, supporting others, especially managers, in their staff development function by providing advice, consultancy and resources has become necessary. The manager may well wish to call upon the assistance of the training officer when identifying resources for staff development – or indeed, at earlier stage in the process. Pepper[16] suggests the notion of *notifiable* and *non-notifiable* training: notifiable training is that which requires resources beyond those available to the manager; non-notifiable training is that which the manager and staff will carry out between them.

I find the matrix (in Figure 5.3) helpful to identify the range of learning and development resources.

But how are these resources to be employed? What are the principles which guide our choice as to the most appropriate methods to be used? For the sake of convenience, this question is addressed in the next section.

Planning

It is not possible to enter the planning phase of staff development without some consideration of adult learning theory. But it is such a vast area of knowledge that it defies description in a few paragraphs. I shall not attempt to summarise it, but to suggest three strands which might be helpful for managers.

Learning style
Just as all of us develop management styles – preferred or patterned behaviour – so we all develop preferred learning styles. Honey and Mumford[17] have developed the work of Kolb[18], and classified these

Figure 5.3

FORMAL

eg induction coaching guiding instructing unit training consultancy critical incident analysis	eg courses and programmes conferences seminars management supervision consultant supervision appraisal job rotation job shadowing team meetings team building action learning guided reading
ON-THE-JOB	OFF-THE-JOB

eg problem-solving
informal feedback
conversations
guiding
coaching
	eg visits
	membership of working
	    parties
	reading
	thinking
	think-tanks
	conversations with peers and
	    colleagues
	support groups

INFORMAL

into four basic types: the *activist*, the *reflector*, the *theorist*, and the *pragmatist*. Each style has its own strengths and weaknesses; each is more or less developed in all of us; most learning activities require the use of all four styles at some stage in the process if change in behaviour is to result.

The activist in us:

– Thrives on new experience
– Is open-minded
– Tackles problems enthusiastically

but

– Is easily bored during the implementation stage

- Tends to hog attention.

The reflector in us:

- Likes to think, observe, listen, reflect
- Enjoys research and analysis
- Prefers structured learning

but

- Tends to dislike the limelight
- Is oppressed by time-pressure.

The theorist in us:

- Prefers to learn through concepts, systems and models
- Enjoys analysis of complex problems
- Emphasises rationality and logic

but

- Dislikes activities which emphasise emotions and feelings
- Is intolerant of activities considered shallow or gimmicky.

The pragmatist in us:

- Likes to see a direct link between learning and practice
- Enjoys trying out new skills
- Emphasises action-planning and implementation

but

- Dislikes theoretical or conceptual material
- Is intolerant of those who wish to explore and think.

Honey and Mumford suggest that managers should become acquainted not only with the preferred learning styles of their staff, but also with their own. For there are activist managers, reflector managers and so on. Finding learning activities which are congruent with both learner and manager will make for effective staff development. Recognising the strengths of team members will help to ensure that strategies for development are carried through.

Experiential learning

Experiential learning is a term much used in youth and community work. The debt owed to John Dewey[19] is not always acknowledged, but much of the modern thinking is derived from his work. Kolb's

well known description of the learning cycle describes the process of
learning experientially (see Figure 5.4 below).

The connection between Kolb's work and that of Honey and
Mumford is clear: four kinds of ability are needed for effective
learning to take place: active, reflective, theoretical and practical.
These abilities take the learner around the learning cycle, from
experience to experience. In designing learning, each stage must be
passed through if behaviour is to change – that is, if practice is to
develop.

Action learning

Action learning, based upon the work of Reg Evans[20], is another
experiential model. It starts with the assumption that the best people
to solve work problems are those who are facing them: that the most
effective learning occurs when people are helped to use their own
experience and skills to solve real issues and problems, and, in doing
so, can extend those skills to tackle new problems as they arise.

The classical action learning model involves bringing together a
'set' of four or five people facing similar work problems and, with the

Figure 5.4

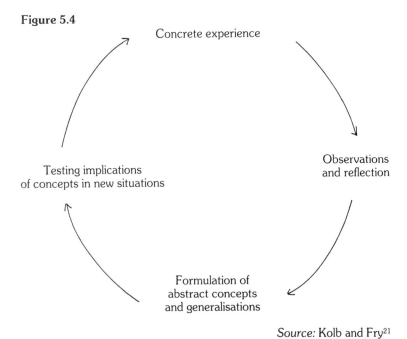

Source: Kolb and Fry[21]

aid of a facilitator or consultant, enabling them to learn from one another in finding solutions. Although originally designed for use with managers, the process is highly relevant to many other situations, including its use by managers with staff groups.

It is a simple model which uses the cycle of experiential learning to create change. Typically, it will involve the following steps:

Step 1 Identify the problem. Is it significant? Who needs to work on it? What are their preferred learning styles?
How can they best be brought together? Who might be the best person to facilitate?
Step 2 The reflection stage. How do we experience the problem? Is it the real problem or do we need to reinterpret?
What questions do we need to ask? Of whom? Are we committed to tackling it?
Step 3 How do we understand the problem? Is it similar to others? What are the alternative solutions? What might be the consequences of each? Do any of the solutions seem worth pursuing? What action would that entail? By whom? When? What help is needed?
Step 4 Try out the solutions. Observe the consequences. What effects were there? On others? On me?
Step 5 What have I learned? About the problem? About others? About me? Return to Step 2. What are the consequences? For the problem? For me?

What are the consequences for managers of these three strands of adult learning? For me, they are the principles upon which many staff development activities can be built. They inform the design of induction, supervision, appraisal, team meetings, working parties and so on. They involve the use of expertise both within the staff group – staff themselves; and they invite the manager to identify resources outside the staff group: non-managerial supervisors, consultants or trainers.

Many of the activities based upon these principles will be planned and deliberate, whilst others will occur spontaneously, in the course of everyday activities and as opportunities present themselves. Every intervention by the manager contains the potential for learning: a question raised and answered; an interpretation of organisation policy offered; a casual sharing of ideas and perceptions. Such seemingly insignificant incidents, added together, form a large proportion of the manager's time spent with staff. Informal 'teaching', as Pepper[22] states 'is an integral part of the day's business and the day's communications and cannot be distinguished from everything else that is going on, except by those who directly experience it as and when it happens'.

Organising and developing

Having discussed the range of staff development opportunities available for managers to use – formal and informal, planned and spontaneous, on and off-the-job – the next phase of the management cycle involves decisions about how to organise and develop them to best effect.

This will very much depend upon the number of staff for whom the manager has responsibility, and on the frequency of contact. It has long been accepted that no one person can manage more than six to eight people. Beyond that number, direct responsibility has to be delegated to others if management is to remain effective. In youth and community work it is frequently exceeded and made more difficult by the location of staff and the part-time nature of much of their involvement.

Putting those difficulties to one side, however, the manager will still wish to organise staff development to best effect. Three principles might assist: firstly, delegating tasks to others not only assists the manager, but provides an opportunity for others to widen their experience (a staff development opportunity in itself); secondly, many staff development opportunities exist outside the manager's direct reach, but can be brought into play by judicious use of consultants, peers and networks of colleagues; and thirdly, given the right encouragement, many staff can and will organise their own opportunities – design their own climbing frames.

Taking care of the climate – ensuring that opportunities for learning are created, that time is put aside, that staff learn how to learn – is a major part of the management task. Supervision, appraisal, team meetings and so on, are all appropriate times both for learning to occur, and for learning to be organised: what learning is needed now? who needs to be involved? how will it happen? what help is required from me or others? when and how shall we review it?

Every manager needs a staff development strategy which identifies the opportunities available, the opportunities which need to be created, the methods to be used, and the resources available and needed. Based on sound learning theory, it will also need to take careful account of personal and job development needs, many of which will be organised around the needs of individual members of staff; and of organisation development needs; many of these will be met through activities organised around groups and teams.

Monitoring, adjusting and evaluating

Staff development strategies and activities, like any other, require the manager to ensure that they continue to be relevant and helpful, are achieving the purposes identified, and represent the best use of resources.

Monitoring and evaluating are concerned with just that: enabling decisions to be made about the adjustment of on-going activity, and about how to do it better next time round. Some evaluation will be concerned with outcomes: what has been achieved? how has practice improved – did it achieve our objectives? was it worth the time and effort? Evaluation should also be concerned with process: who has the activity involved? how did they respond? what really happened?

Building monitoring and evaluation into staff development need not take a great deal of time (has this supervision been useful to you? what did I achieve? has this staff meeting been helpful? how could we improve?), but is essential if activities are to remain relevant. Furthermore, the discipline of including evaluation as part of any strategy should ensure that the views and feeling of staff are taken into account when decisions are made about the future.

I find Hamblin's hierarchy of training effects helpful in developing monitoring and evaluation:

Reaction effects
 – How did we respond or feel?
 – What was intended?

Learning effects
 – What did we learn?
 – What was intended?

Job effects
 – How has practice been affected?
 – What was intended?

Organisation effects
 – How has the organisation benefitted?
 – What was intended?

Ultimate effects
 – What have been the human/social/moral/political effects?
 – What was intended?

(adapted from Hamblin: *The Evaluation and Control of Training)*[23]

Conversations and conclusions

This chapter has attempted to present, in a digestible form, some of the conceptual material available to us – youth officers, full-time workers, part-time or voluntary staff – in our role as managers and developers of the staff for whom we have responsibility.

It invites managers to use it as the basis for their own learning and development: to reflect upon their practice, to conceptualise from that and begin to plan and develop strategies for the development of others.

If the material has a single thread running through it, it is that the manager has a key (perhaps the key) role to play in staff development, as the principal provider of a climate in which learning, growth and development can occur. It invites managers to be active rather than passive, to be systematic rather than opportunistic in their task as agents of personal, job and organisational growth.

At the heart of the manager's strategy lie the conversations that she or he has with individuals and groups of staff. Some of these will be casual or spontaneous encounters; others demand a more planned and considered approach. All require the manager to practice well-known helping skills: listening, reflecting, summarising, clarifying, confronting, contracting. These core skills, used in open and honest conversations, enable the essential elements of good management and staff development to be achieved:

- Re-affirmation and clarification of the standards of work expected and the responsibilities it entails
- Positive and critical feedback about performance, based on accurate information and detailed consideration of past and present
- Opportunities to explore feelings, opinions and ideas
- Opportunities for agreeing plans, targets or goals.[24]

Staff development rarely happens accidentally; and few of us possess the range of knowledge, skills and attitudes which will ensure that we create and use the potential for growth which is present in all people and all organisations. It goes without saying that managers need staff development too. And yet, in 1987, few organisations in the youth and community work field seem prepared to invest the resources required to develop their managers. Many are offered little induction, vague or unrealistic job descriptions, inadequate supervision and few opportunities for in-service training. We have been exhorted to improve the management of the service, but as yet, the resources have not been created with which to do it.

Guidelines to a staff development policy has, I believe, proved to be a useful tool in helping the youth and community service to step beyond its simple concern with training evident in the 1970s to a more holistic approach to the development of staff. It remains for us to explore other approaches and to build from that experience. The guidelines rest upon the premise that organisations will develop through the development of individuals and their jobs. I certainly believe that to be true: the development of managers is a case in point. But it is only part of the picture, for the converse is also true:

that individuals can and do develop through the development of the organisations of which they are part. Both approaches are necessary to improve our work with young people, and both are the legitimate concern of officers and other managers of youth and community work.

References

1. (1985) *Guidelines to a Staff Development Policy*, Council for Education and Training in Youth and Community Work.
2. Main, A (1985), *Educational Staff Development*, Croom Helm.
3. Handy, C (1976), *Understanding Organisations*, Penguin (see also Handy, C (1979), *Gods of Management*, Pan.)
4. Harrison, R (1975), Diagnosing Organisation Ideology, *Annual Handbook for Group Facilitators*, University Associates Publications.
5. Marken, M, Payne, M (1987), *Enabling and Ensuring*, National Youth Bureau and Council for Education and Training in Youth and Community Work.
6. McGregor, D (1960), *The Human Side of Enterprise*, McGraw Hill.
7. See for example Handy, C (1976), (ibid), Chapter 4.
8. Pepper, A D (1984), *Managing the Training and Development Function*, Gower.
9. Maslow, A (1954), *Motivation and Personality*, Harper and Row.
10. Herzberg, F (1966), *Work and the Nature of Man*, World Publishing.
11. Mager, R F, Pipe, P (1984), *Analysing Performance Problems*, David S Lake, California.
12. Heron, J (1973), *Experimental Training Techniques*, Department of Adult Education, University of Surrey.
13. Jardine, M (1987), *From Strength to Strength*, National Youth Bureau and Northern Ireland Association of Youth Clubs.
14. (1984) *Management and Evaluation*, National Youth Bureau.
15. National Group for Trainers (1983), *Trainers in Youth and Community Services: Their Roles, Core Competencies and Training Needs*, National Youth Bureau.
16. Pepper, A D (1984), (ibid).
17. Honey, P and Mumford, A (1986), *The Manual of Learning Styles*, Peter Honey, Maidenhead.
18. Kolb, D A (1984), *Experiential Learning*, Prentice Hall.
19. Dewey, J (1933), *How We Think*, De Heath, Boston, Mass.
20. See for example Revans, R (1983), *The ABC of Action Learning*, Chartwell – Bratt.
21. Kolb, D A, Fry, R (1975), Towards an Applied Theory of Experiential Learning in Cooper, C L, *Theories of Group Processes*, John Wiley.
22. Pepper, A D (1984), (ibid).
23. Hamblin, A C (1974), *The Evaluation and Control of Training*, McGraw Hill.
24. Adapted from unpublished papers for a seminar entitled *Management Menus*, Northern Ireland Association of Youth Clubs and Industrial Training Service Ltd.

6 Legal and personnel matters

John Wood

Whether one views the law as an essential bastion of democracy or shares with Mr. Bumble the less charitable view that the law is an ass will probably depend on whether in any of its aspects it appears to be protecting or curtailing one's freedom.

In trying to maintain this balance the law may be simple or complex. Often it enters into strange contortions in its attempts to do so. It may make exceptions for certain parts of the country to allow for special circumstances or allow room in certain areas for local authorities to exercise their own discretion.

Any attempt to explore legal matters which may be of particular reference to youth officers is therefore fraught with difficulty. Furthermore, within the limitations of one chapter there are matters which can only be skimmed lightly or omitted altogether, for one way or another there are legal implications for all aspects of the officer's work. For these reasons this look at the law does not purport to be anything other than a guide. For authoritative legal advice officers should not hesitate to consult the relevant act, more senior and experienced colleagues or the legal department of their authority or organisation.

On the grounds that the youth officer is primarily engaged in relating to adult workers as trainer, manager, supervisor, counsellor or friend, it is considered important to focus particularly on personnel matters. Attention is also devoted, however, to other aspects of the law with which the youth officer should have a working knowledge in order to be able to offer intelligent advice to workers.

Personnel matters

The statutory basis for the Youth Service is contained in Sections 41 and 53 of The Education Act 1944. The discretion available to local authorities in interpreting their responsibilities under this Act leads to wide differences in the nature and level of provision throughout the country. In local authorities which are subject to changes in political control the youth officer may be required to implement changes in policy with which (s)he may personally agree or disagree and his/her advice may or may not be accepted. Frustrating though this may be the legal wishes of the employer are required to be carried out provided they are reasonable and within the terms of the contract with the employee.

The conditions of service generally applicable to youth officers employed by local authorities are negotiated in the Soulbury Committee. This is the national committee which determines the salary scales and service conditions of inspectors, organisers and advisory officers of local education authorities. The report is frequently adopted also by national voluntary youth organisations as the basis on which they employ their full-time officers. Copies and updates can be obtained from the Local Authorities Conditions of Service Advisory Board (LACSAB) who will advise current subscription rates.

The Soulbury Report relates to such matters as salary scales and grievance procedures but with regard to detailed conditions of service it states simply that these shall be not less favourable than those contained in the scheme of conditions of service for local authorities' administrative, professional, technical and clerical services. These cover such matters as leave entitlement and travel and subsistence allowances but as many employers, whether local authority or voluntary organisations, may interpret the detail of these conditions differently it is important for the youth officer to be familiar with the arrangements determined by their particular employer.

This is just one reason why the careful induction of newly appointed youth officers is essential in both their own interests and those of the employing agency. It is during the induction period that time must be allowed for the new officer to be acquainted with the employer's policy, financial standing orders, administrative procedures, communications and job expectations as well as effecting introductions to other key personnel with whom professional relationships have to be maintained.

Legislation governing employment is contained in the Employment Protection (Consolidation) Act 1978. This Act brought together previous legislation on redundancy pay, contracts of employment and employment protection. It provides that not later than 13 weeks after commencement of employment the employee must be given a written statement which:

1. Identifies the parties to the employment contract and the date of commencement.
2. States the rate of remuneration, intervals of remuneration, title of the job, terms and conditions relating to hours, holidays, sickness, pensions and period of notice.
3. Specifies disciplinary procedures, appeal arrangements, availability of documentation on these matters and whether a contracting out certificate is in force, which allows certain specific exceptions to trade union legislation by joint agreement.

Every employee has the right not to be unfairly dismissed and to appeal to an industrial tribunal if (s)he considers this to be the case.

For the part-time paid and voluntary staff on whom the youth service relies so heavily, there are no nationally agreed conditions or salary scales. These are determined by employers and consequently vary widely across the country. Those employed for less than 16 hours a week have no protection against unfair dismissal unless they have been working for eight hours a week or more for a continuous period of five years. Most employers recognise, however, that it is not in their interest to treat part-time staff in the cavalier fashion which this absence of legal protection might allow.

Full-time workers, on the other hand, are normally employed in accordance with the terms and conditions of the Joint Negotiating Committee for Youth and Community Workers (the JNC Committee). The report of this committee identifies qualifications, conditions of service, salary scales, grievance procedures and probation arrangements. Youth officers should familiarise themselves with this report. As with the Soulbury Report, copies and updates can be obtained from the Local Authorities Conditions of Service Advisory Board.

The Employment Protection Act 1978 as amended by the Employment Acts of 1980 and 1982 includes legislation to safeguard an employee's rights in relation to trade union activities and regulations in respect of closed shops. Under these requirements employees must be allowed reasonable time off during working hours to take part in union activities without pay. Officials of trade unions recognised by the employer are entitled to reasonable time off with pay. Determination as to what is reasonable is normally reached as a result of discussion between the employer and the union but if this proved impossible the employee could complain to an industrial tribunal to obtain a judgement.

Employees must also be allowed reasonable time off without pay to undertake duties as JPs or members of local authority councils. These are minimum provisions and local agreements may exist which improve upon them. Under the act, female employees who meet certain requirements have two statutory rights in connection with absence from work as a result of pregnancy. These are the right to maternity pay and the right to return to work, both of which are conditional on the employee having at least two years continuous service by the beginning of the eleventh week before the expected week of confinement. The significance of this date means that the employee must obtain from her doctor or midwife a certificate confirming the expected date of confinement. The employee's contract of employment must still be in force at the beginning of the eleventh week. A second essential condition is that the employee should give at least 21 days notice of the intended absence and if she intends to return to work this notice must be in writing and state the intention to do so. The right to return applies up to 29 weeks after the date of confinement and the employee is required to give 21 days written notice of her expected return date.

In case the detail of these provisions has been modified by national or local agreements employees should obtain advice from a union, professional association or employer to confirm local conditions and arrangements to ensure that she does not forfeit her rights by failing to meet the necessary requirements.

Several other acts impinge on employment and personnel matters about which the youth officer should be aware. The Social Security and Housing Benefits Act 1982 places responsibility for paying sickness benefit on employers for periods of absence up to 28 weeks in respect of employees with average weekly earnings above a specified minimum, and subject to certain other conditions. It is important that all new employees are informed of the procedures to be followed in the case of absence from work due to sickness. Employing agencies should be able to supply a leaflet or memorandum setting out the procedures to follow in case of sickness but a leaflet, *Employers' Guide to Statutory Sick Pay*, can be obtained from the Department of Health and Social Security. The Rehabilitation of Offenders Act 1974 provides that in most areas of employment people may not be obliged to disclose a 'spent' conviction on an application form and it is unlawful for employers to discriminate against employees as a consequence of such convictions. The Act specifies the rehabilitation periods which must elapse before a conviction is 'spent', according to the nature of the sentence. Exempt from this requirement however are employees concerned with the provision to persons under the age of 18 of accommodation, care, leisure and recreation, schooling, supervision or training whose employment enables them to have access to such persons in the course of their duties. In these cases, convictions are not considered 'spent' and must be declared. Such convictions may constitute grounds for dismissal or refusing someone employment in such posts.

In a further attempt to safeguard children and young people the Department of Education and Science in concert with other Government departments issued *Circular 4/86*. This followed a review by the government of the situations in which known offenders can gain access to young children, and was undertaken as a result of grave public concern arising from specific cases. The circular outlines procedures for the screening of local authority staff. These apply to applicants for voluntary, full-time and part-time paid positions with local authorities who will have substantial access to children up to the age of 16 and young people over 16 who continue at school or suffer from mental or physical handicap. It specifically includes those engaged in the Youth Service. In determining whether access is substantial it is necessary to consider whether the position involves one-to-one contact, is supervised, is isolated, provides opportunities for regular contact or is with particularly vulnerable groups.

The procedure for screening provides for police checks to be sought through a senior nominated officer of the local authority with the permission of the applicant. In making the request a list must be provided of any convictions, bind-over orders or cautions. It should be made clear that if an applicant refuses to give permission for a check to be made this could prevent further consideration of the application. The senior nominated officer may exercise discretion to ensure that the system is not misused or overloaded and will place requests for checks in priority according to the overall demand. Police checks must not under any circumstances take the place of normal diligent recruitment procedures and they should not be used to screen all applicants for a short list.

On receipt of a police report it is up to the local authority to use its judgement to determine whether or not to confirm an appointment. Full details are contained in the DES Circular but arrangements for following the screening procedures and identifying the senior nominated officer will be the subject of more specific advice in each local authority. Arrangements for screening workers employed by voluntary youth organisations are also under consideration.

The Sex Discrimination Act 1975 and the Race Relations Act 1976 make it illegal to discriminate against people on grounds of race or sex, either directly or indirectly, in such matters as recruitment or continuity of employment. Dismissal of a female employee on grounds associated with pregnancy, for example, could constitute sex discrimination.

Exceptions are permitted in certain specific circumstances. Where, for example, a person's occupation requires him or her to enter the presence of persons who are in a state of undress or using sanitary facilities, reasons of decency may require the presence of members of the same sex to be employed for this purpose. Exceptions under the Race Relations Act are also quite specific but they do allow for employees who are required to provide personal services to a racial group which promote their welfare and can be most effectively provided by a person of that same racial group. It is, however, unlawful to publish an advertisement which conveys an intention to discriminate on racial grounds.

The Commission for Racial Equality has published a Code of Practice which has been approved by Parliament and recommends that employers should:

1. Develop an equal opportunities policy.
2. Ensure that personnel selection, practices and policies are monitored and assessed in order to achieve equality.
3. Take positive action to encourage groups which are under-represented to apply for vacancies and/or promotion.

The code came into effect on 1st April, 1984, and can be purchased from the Commission for Racial Equality, who can also supply a very helpful information leaflet. Further advice can also be sought from The Institute of Personnel Management and the Equal Opportunities Commission who will be willing to supply details of leaflets and other publications which are available.

So far we have looked at the way in which legislation affects the appointment and employment of personnel but the youth officer may find him/herself either the subject or the instigator of disciplinary or even dismissal proceedings, and it is therefore important to be aware of the code of practice which should apply in these circumstances. The principal recommendations made by the Advisory, Conciliation and Arbitration Service in this respect are as follows:

1. The specific concern about conduct or capability should be stated in writing identifying clearly to whom it applies.
2. The issue should be dealt with promptly and notice should be given of the possible course of disciplinary action.
3. The roles of different management levels should be identified in the course of disciplinary proceedings and it should be clearly understood that immediate superiors do not normally have authority to dismiss.
4. An individual who is the subject of a complaint should be informed and given the opportunity to present his or her case before decisions are reached.

5. The individual should be given the right to be accompanied by a trade union representative or a friend.
6. Except in the event of gross misconduct an employee should not be dismissed for a first breach of discipline.
7. No disciplinary action should be taken until the case has been thoroughly investigated.
8. Individuals who are to be the subject of disciplinary action should be given a full explanation, told the procedures to be followed, the rights available to them and the procedures for appeal.

Common sense may seem to dictate clearly the course of events but there is a grave danger that it does not always prevail with normal clarity when emotions are generated by personnel problems. By and large, therefore, the steps which should be followed if a significant shortcoming is not rectified are as follows:

1. Give the individual an informal warning at an early stage when the shortcoming has been identified and concern needs to be expressed. This presupposes some evidence or written record which forms the basis on which specific lapses can be identified and discussed.
2. If there is inadequate improvement, issue a formal oral warning in the presence of another senior officer of the employing agency. For this purpose the individual should be told the purpose of the interview beforehand and given the opportunity to be accompanied by a friend or trade union representative.
3. If there is still inadequate improvement, a similar interview procedure should be followed by a more senior officer. This in turn should be followed by a formal written warning identifying the matters on which improvement is required and the period allowed for such improvement before dismissal procedures may be initiated.
4. If there is still inadequate improvement, a disciplinary committee will then be convened by the employing agency.

In all this it should be remembered that the object of the exercise is to improve the professional performance of the employee and help him/her to make an effective contribution to the work of the employing agency. Maximum support must be given to the employee to achieve this objective and the youth officer or other senior officer must be able to specify how that support has been given.

In the event of gross misconduct or criminal liability, it may be necessary for the employer to take peremptory action to suspend an employee pending the outcome of enquiries or proceedings.

Health and safety

One very important piece of legislation which concerns both employees and members of youth and community groups is the Health and Safety at Work Act 1974. It is important that youth officers are alert to the provisions of this act for their role as observers and advisers in the course of visits to organisations could be of vital significance in preventing injury or saving life.

The object of the Act is to reduce accidents and improve health and safety arrangements. To this end it is the duty of all employees, while at work, to take reasonable care of the health and safety of themselves and other persons who may be affected by their actions, and to co-operate with the employing agency to comply with the terms of the Act. Responsibility for enforcing the statutory requirements rests with the Health and Safety Executive from whom further information can be obtained. Most youth officers will find that the local authority's Safety Officer will be only too pleased to give help and advice and assist in offering appropriate and very important training for workers in youth and community groups.

The schedule of potential dangers and precautions called for in working with young people is enormous. To avoid being guilty of neglect under the provisions of the Health and Safety at Work Act requires vigilance, common sense and good communications. All involved should appreciate the importance of identifying and sharing with colleagues and senior officers any concern they may have about health and safety arrangements in the organisation or its activities. The following is a brief check-list of some of the things which the youth officer should be alert to in the context of this legislation:

1. Have the workers received and understood the policies, arrangements and requirements determined by their employers in regard to Health and Safety at Work?
2. Have the workers been given and taken the opportunity to undertake appropriate training?
3. Are fire precautions satisfactory in respect of adequate and operational fire extinguishers; clear access through escape routes and exits; familiarity with the location and use of extinguishers; the provision of a regular maintenance and inspection contract; the operation of a secondary lighting system; the display of clear notices stating action to be taken in the event of fire; familiarisation drills; insulation properties of materials used for furniture, curtains and other furnishings; the use of fire retardent materials on staircases?
4. Are safety guards provided on machinery in workshop or craft areas?

5. Are first-aid boxes kept replenished, and do they include a list of contents?
6. Have any proposed building or electrical alterations been approved and subsequently inspected by properly qualified personnel?
7. Have any unauthorised alterations to wiring been undertaken and are there any trailing cables, damaged switches or faulty connections?
8. Are there any hazards as a result of slippery floors, badly lit passages, uneven or broken surfaces?
9. Are there any fire or health hazards likely as a result of storing inflammable materials or other supplies?
10. Are there any potential dangers as a consequence of glass surfaces, projections or sharp edges relative to the activities being undertaken?
11. Are hand rails, bannisters, cooking appliances safe?

The list could go on and nobody can reasonably expect the youth officer to be an expert on all of these matters. That is why it is important to arrange a regular cycle of safety checks by safety officers and fire officers. Nevertheless, for staff engaged in a youth and community group, the gradual deterioration of surroundings, sheer familiarity with them, and apprehension that a report will only require yet more expenditure, are all very good reasons for the youth officer to look frankly and objectively at health and safety issues. A further piece of legislation relevant in this context is the Reporting of Injuries, Diseases and Dangerous Occurrences Regulations 1985. This requires employers to notify the enforcing authorities, normally the Health and Safety Executive, of (a) fatalities and (b) accidents which result in more than three days incapacity, or major injury. Local authorities and other large employers will have their own accident reporting arrangements and youth officers should familiarise themselves with them. Some parts of the regulations refer only to accidents to employees in the course of their work. Fatal or major injury accidents which involve any person, however, must all be reported by the quickest possible means, such as telephone, and followed up by a written report.

Many activities conducted under the aegis of the Youth Service are recognised as carrying a high risk which can be exacerbated as a result of unusual circumstances or inexperienced supervision. Youth Officers may be directly involved as leaders or instructors but are more likely to be involved in condoning or approving the appointment of other responsible staff. Even if not thus involved, the officer must always be vigilant to ensure that all reasonable care has been taken to secure the safety of those engaged in the activity. High on the priority list must be confidence that the person in charge holds qualifications and experience relative to the level of activity being undertaken, whether using power tools or weight training equipment, taking part in sport or engaging in outdoor adventure pursuits.

Governing bodies of sport can often advise on the qualifications which are appropriate to different levels of activity. Local Authority Education Departments may also be able to offer advice, and the Department of Education and Science's booklet, *Safety in Outdoor Pursuits*, also contains much useful advice. The youth officer may sometimes be faced with a dilemma in this aspect of the work, for so dependent is the youth service on the enthusiastic amateur that one may be reluctant to cause offence by casting doubt on workers' competence. This inhibition, coupled with a worker's dedication and enthusiasm, can cloud an objective assessment of his or her capabilties. For this reason it must be clearly explained to all concerned that the employing agency has specific requirements which do not allow instructors to carry responsibility for certain levels of activity without holding an appropriate qualification. Probably the most common example of this policy is the prohibition which attaches to the use of school gymnasium apparatus other than by a qualified PE teacher. Another is the requirement that staff responsible for taking young people into wild country must hold a Mountain Leadership Certificate, and it must be recognised at the same time that this, on its own, is not regarded as adequate for offering instruction in, for instance, rock climbing.

Safety must be of paramount importance, too, when organisations organise specific stunts or fund-raising events such as marathon walks or runs. It is important that youth officers insist on consultation with the police or other relevant authorities if routes impinge in any way on traffic routes or recreation areas.

Young people and the law

The youth officer is not expected to be a legal expert or consultant, but must be in a position to tap into appropriate sources from which advice can be obtained, be generally aware of relevant legislation, offer training to personnel engaged in youth and community work and generally use the experience acquired over the years in the interests of young people and their social education.

Nowhere is this more true than in respect of the law as it affects young people. This is a lengthy and complex subject. Helpful literature on this and on The Police and Criminal Evidence Act 1984 can be obtained from the National Youth Bureau. Some aspects, on which the youth officer should have a general working knowledge in order to respond to queries from youth workers, are referred to briefly in the following notes, including: police interviews with young people; the co-operation expected of youth workers; police powers to stop and detain; and the law as it affects young people in respect of tobacco, alcohol, solvent abuse and drugs.

Judges Rules indicate that interviews with young people under 17 should only be conducted in the presence of a parent or guardian or, in their absence, a person other than a police officer, who is of the same sex as the child or young person. If the police insist on conducting an interview on youth group premises, the worker can insist upon the presence of a member of staff who should ensure that any information given by the young person is done so freely, and on the basis that the interviewee will not thereby be incriminated. If the police officer refuses to co-operate in this way, the worker should note the officer's number and notify his employing agency of the full circumstances.

There is no obligation to disclose information to the police that could incriminate anybody, nor is it an offence to decline to answer questions asked by a police officer. It would, however, be an offence to take any action to destroy or conceal evidence or enter any kind of arrangement which might be deemed to impede or pevert the course of justice. In determining whether or not to disclose information, the issue has to be faced honestly, for it may mean that a moral obligation towards the community and respect for law and order must be balanced carefully against the interests of the individual.

The Police and Criminal Evidence Act gives the police considerable powers to stop, search, arrest, interrogate and detain, provided there are reasonable grounds for suspicion. In this connection, prohibited articles, for which a search may be made, include offensive weapons and articles intended to cause injury. A pocket knife or even keys could be included in this description. Other prohibited articles are those which could be used to break the law, such as skeleton keys, gloves to conceal fingerprints or plastic cards.

An arrest can be made for such actions as burglary, criminal damage, indecent assault, taking a car, aiding and abetting an offence, or if the police have reasonable grounds for suspicion. The police also have a general power to arrest if, for example, it is impracticable or inappropriate to serve a summons, or on their failure to find or believe the suspect's name or address, or for obstruction of the highway, or to protect persons or property. Under the Act, the police also have powers to take the fingerprints of young people over the age of 10 without parental consent if it is considered likely that this will prove or disprove their involvement in a criminal offence, or if the person has been charged, convicted or told that (s)he will be reported for an offence.

Another aspect of the law with which the youth officer should have a general working knowledge concerns young people and their use or abuse of tobacco, alcohol, solvents and drugs and the following notes are relevant in this connection:

1. While it is not an offence for children under 16 to buy tobacco, it is an offence under the Children & Young Persons Act 1933 to sell it to them. It is also contrary under Section 7 of this Act for persons under 16 to smoke in public.

2. It is an offence under the Licensing Act 1964 to sell alcohol to people under 18.

    Under 14 a young person is not permitted in a public house. Between 14 and 16 the landlord may allow them in the public house but they cannot buy or drink liquor there.

    Between 16 and 18 they may buy and consume beer, cider, porter or perry (but not wine or spirits) with a meal on licensed premises.

    Children over the age of five and people under 16 can drink beer, wine or even spirits so long as they are not in a bar and the drink is not bought by them.

    For a juvenile to be found drunk in public is a criminal offence.

3. It is not illegal to sell, buy, possess or sniff solvents except that the Intoxicating Substance (Supply) Act 1985 makes it an offence to knowingly supply people under 18 with any substance likely to be inhaled or cause intoxication. Unruly or offensive behaviour resulting from solvent abuse may lead to arrest under other regulations, such as causing a breach of the peace.

4. Under the Misuse of Drugs Act 1971 it is a criminal offence to manufacture, possess, supply or offer to supply a controlled drug. It is also a criminal offence to allow premises which one owns or manages to be used for the illicit supply of controlled drugs. If there are reasonable grounds for suspicion a police officer may enter premises without a search warrant in order to question or search suspects, and it is an offence to intentionally obstruct an officer from carrying out these powers. The owner or manager of the premises can, however, legally require a search warrant if (s)he wishes, before a search for drugs can be undertaken on the premises.

    Controlled drugs include heroin, cocaine, morphine, diconal, pethidine, cannabis, codeine, amphetamine and other amphetamine-based drugs.

    Anybody who knows or suspects that somebody is a drug addict is under no legal obligation to report the matter, or to report suspected possession of drugs. There is a legal obligation on doctors, however, to inform the Home Office if they have cause to believe that a person is addicted to a controlled drug.

Youth officers should, under these circumstances, be in a position to advise youth workers where to turn for help locally when dealing with a young person who has drug related problems. This may be medical assistance or referral to a specialised agency, following discussion with parents. Any youth worker who knows that drugs are being passed on his/her premises would be in an indefensible legal position if the police were not informed immediately.

Many agencies have literature on the subject of solvents, drugs and alcohol, including the Health Education Authority, the DHSS and the Health and Safety Executive. The first contact, however, should perhaps be the local Health Education Officer.

Transport

In contemporary mobile society youth and community groups rely heavily on motor transport to implement programmes of activity, and as this is an area of the work beset with numerous legal pitfalls, the youth officer should have a good general knowledge of the subject. Relevant legislation is contained in the Minibus Act 1977; The Public Passenger Vehicles Act 1981; The Minibus (Designated Bodies) Order 1980, The Transport Act 1985, and various other acts concerning construction, equipment and conditions of fitness.

The operator of a minibus is the person responsible for its licensing, use and overall operation and to whom the driver is responsible. The operator could be the local authority, a head teacher, a youth worker or a person designated by a management committee. The operator must acquire a permit for either a small passenger vehicle with seats for 9–16 passengers inclusive or for a large passenger vehicle with more than 16 passenger seats. Permit discs must be displayed in the vehicle when it is operating under permit. The driver of a vehicle operating under a permit must hold a full current driving licence, be over 21 years of age and be reasonably experienced.

A permit is not required if an organisation operates a minibus as a privately owned vehicle without an element of 'fare contribution'. This could be taken to preclude contributions from members towards running costs or upkeep of a vehicle through subscription payments. As a consequence, organisations usually prefer to make sure that they keep within the law by meeting the cost of the small fee payable for a permit.

Permits for small passenger-carrying vehicles may be granted to eligible organisations concerned with education, religion, social welfare, recreation, or other activities of benefit to the community, by the Traffic Commissioner or bodies designated by the Secretary of State, which include many of the national voluntary youth organisations and local authorities. Permits for passenger vehicles with more than 16 seats can only be issued by the Traffic Commissioner. These are granted to bodies which co-ordinate group activities of benefit to the community over an area, provided the Commissioner is satisfied about maintenance arrangements.

Vehicles must comply with detailed legislation about their construction, fitness and equipment. It is reasonable to assume that a manufacturer will have met these requirements in respect of standard minibuses bought new or secondhand. Once a vehicle has been acquired the operator must ensure that it continues to comply with the regulations.

The greatest care needs to be taken over the conversion of non-passenger vehicles or conversions undertaken by organisations on a self-help basis. Legislation governing the construction of minibuses is contained in the Road Vehicle (Construction and Use) Regulations 1986 and the Minibus (Conditions of Fitness, Equipment and Use) Regulations 1977 (as subsequently amended). Large passenger carrying vehicles are also required to comply with the Public Service Vehicles (Conditions of Fitness, Equipment, Use and Certification) Regulations 1981. Further advice may be sought on this matter from the National Advisory Unit for Community Transport.

Some specific points to note in connection with the operation of minibuses are as follows:

1. It is illegal for a vehicle fitted with a rear exit to draw a trailer.
2. Overloading or altering or adding a roof rack may breach regulations.
3. Access between seats and exits must be unobstructed.
4. The maximum overall length of a minibus is 7m. and in respect of large passenger vehicles it is 12m.
5. Every minibus must carry a fire extinguisher and first aid box conforming to certain specifications.
6. Windows must be clean and unbroken.
7. Dangerous substances such as camping gaz, petrol or paraffin must be in secure containers such that they cannot cause damage to the passengers or the vehicle in an accident.
8. The vehicle must be taxed and insured.
9. Minibuses with seats for nine passengers or more must be tested annually. Those with seats for 12 or less can be tested by any approved MOT examiner. Those with more than 12 passanger

seats must be tested by an examiner authorised by the Department of Transport.

10. Standing passengers are not permitted.

It is a requirement of EC regulations that tachographs shall be fitted to all vehicles with nine or more passenger seats used outside Great Britain or with 17 or more passenger seats when used wholly in Great Britain. It has been argued that these regulations do not apply to privately-owned and driven vehicles and in 1981 the Minister of Transport affirmed that it is very unlikely that a prosecution would be attempted in this country. He added, however, that it would be for the courts to interpret the law (Hansard, 20th July, 1981).

With effect from 1st April, 1988, the permit regulations and existing conditions of fitness for use applicable to minibuses will be replaced by a revised and unified set of regulations, in respect of all minibuses manufactured on or after 1st October, 1987, and registered after 1st April, 1988.

The use of private cars is another aspect of member conveyance which needs special caution. It is normal practice for employees who use their own cars to convey passengers in the course of their work to be required to indemnify their employer against third party claims. Irrespective of such a requirement it is wise for employees to secure an endorsement on their insurance policy which allows them to use their own vehicle for purposes of business. In the course of youth and community work, however, groups often receive help from members or parents for the conveyance of young people to various events, and under these circumstances workers have a responsibility to ensure that they take every reasonable care to secure the safety of their members. A code of conduct, or policy which organisations may consider, would require that such vehicles are roadworthy and comply with the law, that the driver is qualified and fit to drive, that the driver's insurance offers adequate cover and includes passengers, and that parents are aware of the arrangements and have the opportunity to exclude their children from them.

Financial matters

Whether fund-raising is regarded as a chore or a stimulating activity, most youth and community groups have to undertake it, and voluntary organisations in particular find it an advantage to secure charitable status. This enables them to receive covenanted donations for five or seven years and recover tax paid thereon, and to benefit from the 'Give as Your Earn' scheme. Interest on investments is also tax free and registered charities may be able to claim additional tax relief.

A registered charity has to comply strictly with regulations about keeping accounts and the appointment and duties of trustees. To apply, the organisation must submit to the Commissioners two certified copies of their constitution, details of their objectives and activities, and copies of accounts for each of the three preceding years. It is acceptable to submit a draft constitution with an invitation to the Charity Commissioners to offer comments.

Once registered, audited accounts must be sent to the Charity Commission annually. The Commissioners will not assist with the preparation of documentation but they will help by offering comment, opinion or advice on a charity's activities.

There are two offices. Charities operating south of a line between The Wash and the Bristol Channel refer to London. Those north of that line and in Wales refer to Liverpool. Once registration has been granted the charity should also register with the Inland Revenue in order to obtain tax exemption or recover tax on covenanted income. This is done through the Inland Revenue Claims Branch, to whom a request should be made for exemption extended to registered charities under the terms of the Income and Corporation Taxes Act 1970 and for the relevant claim forms to be supplied.

Among the many different ways of fund-raising, care should be taken not to infringe the law in respect of lotteries and amusements, which are controlled by the Lotteries and Amusements Act 1976.

Exempt from this Act are small lotteries which form part of another entertainment, such as a fête or a dance or sports event, provided that:

1. The whole of the net proceeds of the entertainment, including the lottery, are not devoted to private gain, and that the cost of any prizes charged against the lottery does not exceed £50.
2. None of the lottery prizes are cash prizes.
3. The tickets are only sold and the result declared on the premises during the entertainment.
4. The lottery is not the only or most substantial attraction to the event.

There is another exemption which relates to private lotteries limited to members of a society or people who work or reside at the same place.

Most youth and community groups will be interested only in the small lotteries referred to above as exempt from the Act, or a larger lottery designated as a 'Society's Lottery'. This is subject to the Act and tickets may be sold to a wider public provided the proceeds are not for private gain or commercial undertaking. Organisations wishing to promote such a lottery must register with the local authority and pay an initial registration fee. A further annual fee is then payable on the 1st January. Conditions governing such lotteries are as follows:

1. No prize shall exceed a specified maximum and a maximum is also placed on the price of ticket.
2. Nett proceeds shall be devoted to charitable purposes, athletic sports, games or cultural activities or the purposes for which the society exists.
3. Expenses set against the proceeds shall not exceed the actual expenses incurred or 25% of the total proceeds and the cost of prizes shall not exceed half the total proceeds.
4. The prices of tickets must all be the same and shown on the ticket which must be paid for in full before the draw.
5. There are limits on the total sales value of tickets and the number of lotteries which can be held.
6. A return must be made to the local registration authority within three months and a form will usually be provided for this purpose.

The sale of intoxicating liquor as a contributory fund raiser or complementary facility at events is controlled by the Licencing (Occasional Permissions) Act 1983. This provides that on not more than four occasions per year during a period not exceeding 24 hours an occasional licence to sell intoxicating liquor may be granted to organisations not carried on for the purpose of private gain. To apply for a licence, two copies of a written application should be sent to the clerk of the licensing justices at least a month before the date of the function. The applicant may be required to attend in person. Alternatively, the holder of a justices on-licence may apply for an occasional licence to sell alcoholic drinks at some place other than his/her licenced premises.

Other fund-raising activities which require licences include house-to-house collections, street collections and possibly car boot sales. Application should be made to the local authority who will advise on the relevant procedures and requirements and whether or not permission is required for car boot sales although the conditions of the Local Government (Miscellaneous Provisions) Act 1982 do not generally apply when these are for charitable or sporting purposes.

Insurance

Systems for handling and accounting for money in an organisation are areas of work on which the youth officer is frequently required to advise, and one area in which particular care is required relates to insurance protection. It is an area in which groups may be tempted to be frugal and as a result could find themselves in financial difficulty if, for example, their premises were to be under-insured in the event of fire. Most national voluntary organisations have negotiated special insurance terms and will offer advice and recommendations. Nevertheless, organisations should be aware of the different kinds of insurance and the extent of their cover in respect of buildings, contents, public and employers' liability and personal accident.

Local authorities may cover their own premises and contents against fire risk only. Some policies exclude accidental or malicious damage. Personal accident cover may exclude certain activities or require supplementary premiums for specific events or journeys. In respect of journeys, groups should be advised to inform parents precisely about insurance arrangements and in respect of hazardous activities it may be wise to seek a letter of indemnity from parents acknowledging and consenting to the risks involved. This may give the leader some protection in the event of accidental injury, such as sprains and bruises, but it is extremely doubtful whether it would offer any protection against a charge of negligence in the event of serious injury. Nevertheless, good communication with parents about programmes, projects and activities makes good sense and is particularly important in respect of journeys of any distance or deviation from routine.

Public performances

Under the Local Government (Miscellaneous Provisions) Act 1982, an entertainment licence is required for public dancing, music and most forms of public entertainment. The Act does not apply to Northern Ireland and there are certain exemptions in respect of places of worship, pleasure fairs and certain open-air events.

A licence is not generally required for garden fêtes, sales of work, meetings, debates, quiz shows, plays in which music is only incidental, exhibitions and sporting events, such as athletic meetings. It is required for public events involving such sports as wrestling, boxing or martial arts. If in any doubt as to whether or not a licence is required it is advisable to check with the licencing department of the local authority.

There is no statutory definition of a 'public' entertainment. Generally speaking, members of a private organisation or their guests would not be regarded as members of the public, whether or not an admission fee is charged. To ensure that an entertainment does not become public, tickets should not be generally available on demand, advertising should be limited and admission should be restricted to members and guests who hold invitations. The penalty for infringing the law exposes the organisation and management to a fine on conviction not exceeding £1,000, so it is wise to consult the licencing section of the local authority well in advance. They will advise on safety standards, the charges for either an occasional or an annual licence and whether the authority may be willing to exercise discretion in waiving fees in the case of charitable or educational functions. At least 28 days notice must be given in respect of acquiring, transferring or renewing a licence.

Under the Theatres Act 1968 a licence is required for the public performance of any play or dramatic piece given wholly or in part by live performers and where all or most of the live performance involves playing a role. This includes plays, operas, musical shows, nativity plays and ballet. Guidelines given above as to the definition of Public performances in relation to entertainment licences also apply to the public performance of plays. Safety requirements identified in the licence must be observed. These relate to such matters as lighting, exit routes, fire precautions and seating arrangements. Periods of notice required for a licence as stipulated in the Act are:

> One or more particular occasions: 14 days
> Grant or transfer of a period licence: 21 days
> Renewal of a period licence: 28 days.

Exempt from the need to obtain a licence are private performances of plays and certain religious events such as harvest festivals.

Youth officers should bear in mind when advising youth and community groups that licencing regulations have been introduced not as a revenue-raising exercise or to create a legal obstacle course, but generally to secure the safety of those who attend. That should be at the forefront of consideration, whereupon most people will readily appreciate that when there is any doubt it should be discussed with the licencing department of the local authority, and an application for the relevant licence should be made.

Copyright and performing rights

The protection of original works produced by writers, composers and other artists in England, Scotland and Wales is governed by the Copyright Act 1956. This is a complex and lengthy piece of legislation which is intended to prevent the copying of any piece of work without the author's permission and secure payment of any fee which may be required. This permission is normally sought by reference to the publisher. Royalties payable for permission to perform plays or other works are normally printed inside the front cover of the script or score.

The Act applies to literary, dramatic and musical works and to artistic works such as engravings, photographs, charts, diagrams, paintings and sculptures. It also applies to film, broadcasts, videos, sound recordings and computer programmes.

There is no requirement to register copyright, and even in the absence of the copyright symbol ©, a work may still be protected. There are certain conditions under which material can be copied or performed without permission. If, for example, only an insubstantial extract is copied, in the sense not simply of quantity but in its context within the total work, it is possible that permission may not be necessary. The holder of copyright could, of course, challenge the opinion that it was insubstantial and take legal proceedings. Copyright on literary and dramatic works lapses 50 years after the death of the author or the first publication, whichever is the later. Copyright on photographs and records lasts for 50 years from the date of first publication, irrespective of whether the author is still alive. Care must be exercised in relying on these exclusions. If, for example, a new version of an old recording is produced, it would probably be classified as a new recording. In determining the ownership of copyright, somebody who creates work on behalf of an employer is not entitled to the copyright unless there is a contractual agreement to the contrary. The copyright of a private letter belongs to the writer unless it is sent to a newspaper without stipulating clearly that it is not for publication.

In youth organisations and many community activities, music is a key feature. It should be recognised that to tape an existing recording, even for private use, infringes copyright. It is unlikely, however, that a recording company would proceed against somebody who genuinely records for private use. Any musical performance outside the domestic circle is interpreted as a public performance even, in the case of a youth club, if the audience is confined to club members, irrespective of whether or not there is a charge for admission and irrespective of whether or not the performance is given live or by mechanical means, such as record players, radio, television or tape recorder. Youth and community groups are, therefore, well advised to obtain a licence from the Performing Right Society Ltd to cover their musical activities on an annual basis.

In the case of sound recordings, copyright permission is required as follows:

1. To give a public performance of a record or tape permission should be sought from Phonographic Performances Ltd.

2. To give a public performance of musical works permission should be sought from the Performing Right Society Ltd.

There are therefore two licences which are required by youth and community groups, one which protects the interests of the recording companies and the other which protects the interests of the composers and performers.

Groups which wish to make recordings of tapes or records should obtain permission from the Mechanical Copyright Protection Society. In respect of copying music, some publishers have agreed that they will not institute proceedings if copies are made in certain very specific circumstances. Details of this agreement can be obtained from the Music Publishers' Association in a pamphlet entitled *Fair Copying Rules OK!*

The copyright position on films is very complex and it would be wise to assume that all films are protected, irrespective of age; it may in any event be difficult to trace the owner. Help under these circumstances may be obtained from the British Film Institute.

Another body which may be willing to offer further advice on copyright matters is The Council for Educational Technology, and, with regard to copyright in the music industry, the Performing Rights Society has compiled a helpful list of publications and addresses.

The changing position

Agreements, regulations and laws are constantly changing and being updated. Several, to which reference has been made in this chapter, are currently under review. It is emphasised, therefore, that these notes should not be regarded as anything other than a general guide to some of the legal background to which youth officers should have regard in the context of their work. Hopefully they will enable the reader to proffer constructive advice, and the address list of bodies referred to in this chapter may also prove a useful resource for more comprehensive information and expertise.

If this short voyage of exploration through the legal network has not thrown enough light on a particular matter of concern to the reader further enquiries may be necessary. These could result in discoveries of interest to other officers if passed to professional journals, associations or bodies, such as the National Council for Voluntary Youth Services or the National Youth Bureau, for there are many aspects of this subject on which further illumination could be helpful to those engaged in the Youth and Community Service.

Note: For an address list of organisations referred to in this chapter see Appendix on page 188.

7 Partnership and inter-agency co-operation

David Smith

The youth service is peculiar among services to the public in Britain today in that the overwhelming majority of the provision is still delivered through voluntary effort. Along with social welfare services, mainstream education and others, the organised youth service started with the intervention of public spirited individuals. Unlike the other services, however, central and local government have not taken the lead in youth work in such a way that the state has become the major provider.

It was not until the state perceived a threat to the morals of young people from the blackout and evacuation at the start of World War II that local government was encouraged to become involved in youth work by the *Board of Education Circular 1486*[1] of 1939. By this time, the major voluntary youth organisations, mainly the uniformed and church-based organisations, were well established. Circular 1486 recognised that the Brigades, Scouting and the other established organisations had developed expertise and structures on which local authorities would need to draw if their new venture into youth provision was to be successful. So the Board of Education asked local education authorities to co-operate in this work with the voluntary youth organisations through local youth committees, and the concept of the local youth service partnership was born.

Unfortunately, in many parts of the country, the youth service partnership has progressed no further than the aspirations of Circular 1486. And some areas are still to achieve that level. Partnership is still seen as a way whereby the interests of the local education authority youth service and those of the voluntary organisations can be made to co-exist without too much harm or aggravation being caused to each other. The focus is usually resources; and this is not even interpreted in its broadest meaning, encompassing the human resource of skilled people. Most often it is local authority grant-aid to the voluntary sector, and the means of deciding this, which is interpreted as the youth service partnership.

The youth service partnership could and should be a much broader and more rewarding aspect of the provision than that outlined in Circular 1486. But to achieve this requires an understanding of the concept of partnership, structures which enable it, skills to facilitate it, and methods of working which are not counter-productive to the maintenance of the partnership.

The youth service partnership is one between not just two, but many partners. It can exist at several levels; the national level, the regional level, at local education authority (LEA) area level and at neighbourhood level. For the purposes of this chapter, which is primarily addressed to the youth officer and other youth service 'middle managers', the focus will tend to be the partnership at an LEA area level; but other levels will not be excluded.

First, there is the partnership between individual voluntary youth organisations. This is usually identified as existing through national bodies, such as NCVYS in England, and through local consortia and umbrella bodies, such as local councils for voluntary youth services (CVYSs).

Second, there is the partnership between voluntary youth organisations and the local authority youth service. Where this is formalised, it is often enacted through voluntary sector representation on a local authority youth advisory committee, the successor to Circular 1486's local youth committee.

Third, there is the partnership between young people and the adults who normally control both the local authority and voluntary youth services. Where this involves young people participating in youth service decision-making at more than club or unit level, it is often referred to as the 'three way' partnership.

Last, there is the partnership between central government and the providers of youth service. In the past, central government has preferred to work through local authorities. Developments such as Education Support Grants and Grant Related In-Service Training (GRIST) have highlighted central government's partnership with the local youth service provider.

Inter-agency co-operation differs slightly from partnership in a youth service context. Whereas the latter is where the partners in the provision of youth service work together with each other, and with young people, inter-agency co-operation concerns voluntary youth organisations and local authority youth services working together with those agencies outside youth service which affect the lives of young people.

The pressure which our society places on young people means that many specialist agencies whose prime foci are, for example, social welfare, housing or unemployment, have an increasing concern with young people and their situation. The youth service is well-placed to help co-ordinate this range of services in an attempt to see the young as whole people, rather than as the sum of their special needs.

Why work in partnership?

There is a story in the youth service, probably apocryphal, of the two youth clubs which were built at opposite ends of the same street. The local authority and a voluntary organisation had both noted a need for provision in the area, and had both responded. Unfortunately, the construction of both buildings was too far advanced before the duplication was noticed. The result was two buildings in an area where there was insufficient demand to support both.

Although this may only be a story, there is evidence that such things do happen. A report of research in Liverpool[2] showed that there is a huge mismatch in that city between the location of youth provision and where young people live. Areas with high provision have few young residents and areas with a high youth population are poorly served.

The first reason for working together, then, is to co-ordinate youth work provision. This ranges from agreeing the location of buildings to ensuring that organisation A's fund-raising event does not clash with organisation B's, to the detriment of both.

A second reason for working together in partnership is the need for representation. There is a plethora of agencies which affect the lives of young people and the youth service. Individual organisations or groups of young people could not hope to keep in touch with all these bodies but, if they can develop the machinery and the trust to make it work, one person can represent the rest. So, with the aid of regular support group meetings, the Chair of the British Youth Council can represent the youth service and young people on the Manpower Services Commission's Youth Training Board. And, through the local CVYS, the Guide Commissioner can represent the voluntary youth service on the police liaison committee.

More importantly, partnership processes can help the youth service to identify the changing needs of young people in a changing society, and then help to develop and adapt its provision to meet those needs.

The youth worker who comes across one young person who has left home after a family row and cannot find anywhere to live may respond as if this is simply an individual's personal problem. But when, through some collective forum, the worker learns of a number of similar occurrences, then it becomes clear that there is a young homelessness issue for the service as a whole.

If there is then some means whereby those in the youth service can work together to provide training for youth workers in counselling homeless young people, to encourage local housing authorities to provide accommodation for young single people and to give youth work insights to a local housing association building single person accommodation, then the partnership will really be working.

More commonly, partnership is practised for pragmatic reasons. The local authority has the canoes, but not the trainer for outdoor pursuits training, and so combines effort with the voluntary organisation which has the expertise but not the equipment. Sharing and co-operation over resources are among the most common manifestations of partnership. Unfortunately, this seldom goes beyond cash and equipment to encompass effort and skills.

The last reason for working in partnership relates to the development of the organisation and of the individual within it. The youth service in England is very insular in its nature. The youth service provision of two neighbouring local authorities can vary enormously, as can the way in which the provision is organised. Two apparently similar voluntary organisations can have vastly different ethos, structures and programme. Which is fine if those varying styles come from enlightened, conscious decisions; one of the strengths of youth service is the choices it offers to young people. But if those variations come from a lack of knowledge of the alternatives – 'we do it this way because we have always done it this way' – then there is a stagnation of both thought and action. Written examples of practice are one way to learn from other models, but it is no substitute for learning by personal contact and by working together.

Similarly with the partnership with young people, only by talking with them and involving them can the adult providers of youth service ensure that young people's real needs are met. And only by participation in real decision-making will young people learn from their experience, surely one of the prime aims of the service.

The partnership between voluntary youth organisations

The definition of what is a voluntary youth organisation has become a lot less clear in recent years. When NCVYS was first formed, it brought together the eleven major national voluntary youth organisations of that time[3] and, although this was quickly expanded to involve another eight organisations, there appears to have been little doubt as to what constituted a voluntary youth organisation.

Now, organisations which used to be run almost entirely by volunteers have had to employ increasing numbers of staff to enable them to do their work. There is currently a debate within the Girl Guides Association, an organisation where volunteers still undertake almost all of the tasks, as to whether some of the senior advisory roles should become the work of full-time employees. This recognises the difficulty of recruiting and retaining volunteers for such time-consuming and skilled posts.

As more organisations employ large staffs, one has to ask – what is a voluntary organisation? Is the LEA-maintained youth centre, with a management committee comprising mainly volunteers, a voluntary youth organisation? The answer lies in the primacy and independence of the volunteer in decision-making. If the staff are ultimately responsible to volunteers, then it is a voluntary organisation. Secondly, if the volunteers have the ultimate control of the organisation then, again, it is voluntary. For example, a local authority could eventually close a voluntary youth organisation through the withdrawal of grant aid, but the organisation's voluntary managers could choose to try to continue by raising alternative finance. Whereas if the authority is empowered to close the organisation, in spite of the management committee's protestations, then it is not a voluntary body.

Defining the 'youth' aspect of a voluntary youth organisation is less simple. Research commissioned by the Croydon Guild of Voluntary Organisations[4] has shown that, whereas the Croydon LEA youth service, which was rightly proud of its contact with the voluntary sector, had links with just under 500 voluntary youth organisations in the Borough, there were an additional 500 units which could be described as voluntary youth organisations.

As well as the uniformed, church and club-based organisations, the research found that many specialist organisations with a young membership share the same activities and problems as voluntary youth organisations. Sports, drama, dance and other specialist organisations may all have young people as a large proportion of their memberships and may have similar programmes to youth organisations.

What is the difference between a youth club which runs a five-a-side football game, and a five-a-side football club which attracts young people? Probably very little on the surface.

One way of clarifying which is a youth organisation, is to ask whether or not the organisation is a vehicle for the experiential and social education of the young people, or is it used merely to achieve some other of the organisation's aims, such as winning a competition or providing a leisure pursuit for the young people.

The Croydon research found that a large number of the specialist organisations were actually doing youth work by the above definition, whether they acknowledged it or not. In passing, it might be interesting to ask how many organisations claiming to do youth work through their activities actually achieve this aim. So, the mark of a voluntary youth organisation is more about what organisations try to achieve than what form their activity takes.

The most common machinery whereby voluntary youth organisations come together in partnership in England is the local Council for Voluntary Youth Service, or CVYS. These originated when the local branches of national voluntary youth organisations, in membership of NCVYS, formed their own local equivalent of the national body within a specific LEA area. In 1974, NCVYS acknowledged the existence of these local standing conferences, as they were then known, and gave them the opportunity for equal membership with the national bodies. Currently, there is a CVYS, or equivalent body, in almost all of the Shire counties and in most major cities. Unfortunately, the voluntary sector rarely comes together in a CVYS in the outer Metropolitan districts.

The origin of CVYSs in the coming together of the local branches of the established national voluntary youth organisations (NVYOs) is both their strength and their weakness. It is a strength in that the regional and county level officers of the NVYOs usually provide the main support for the CVYS. They take the role of honorary officers and ensure secretarial and administrative back-up. Some NVYOs actively encourage their staff to be involved in CVYSs, or even to promote one where none exists.

The drawback comes because, firstly, such officers in NVYOs tend to be heavily committed already. If paid officers, they will often have responsibility within their organisation for several LEA areas; this can be quite a large number if the patch includes small, outer Metropolitan districts. If they are volunteers, they may have full-time jobs of their own, as well as some managerial responsibility within their organisation. Such officers can be exhorted to become involved in a CVYS by their own organisation's headquarters, but will only respond if they are given the space in their work-load to carry it through.

Secondly, with CVYSs dominated by established NVYOs, the small, one-off voluntary youth organisations, which were found to comprise almost 50 per cent of the voluntary sector in the Croydon study, may not perceive these umbrella bodies as relevant to their own needs. This may be exacerbated in areas with high black and other ethnic minority populations. The established NVYOs tend to involve the indigenous white population, and ethnic minority youth work tends to be delivered through one-off and community-based organisations. It takes a great deal of concerted effort and trust for both groupings to work together through a single body.

The Croydon report found that a way round this problem may be to replace or supplement the CVYS with a series of informal networks. The one-off groups find the rather formal committee structure of a CVYS, which is natural to those familiar with an established organisation, inappropriate for their needs. The drawbacks with informal networks are that they make the representative function more complex and they require a level of servicing which can only come from a CVYS which can afford full-time staff.

The sharing and co-operative aspects of the partnership between voluntary youth organisations can be most productive if promoted at a more local level than the LEA area. It is easier to share with the club down the road than it is to negotiate a deal between two county-wide groups. Some of this happens naturally through leaders from different organisations knowing each other socially; but busy volunteers rarely have a wide circle of friends outside their own organisation.

Some attempts have been made at promoting this more local partnership between voluntary youth organisations. Two which have had some success have both involved the LEA in an enabling role. Gloucestershire CVYS, which is serviced by the LEA, established a network of sub-committees at area level. However, it has always been difficult to persuade already over-committed volunteers to give up an evening for yet another committee. ILEA overcame this problem to some extent by developing spending powers down to its area youth committees. If you miss the meeting, you don't get a say on spending. Both examples, though, rely on LEA area officers having the skills and time required to facilitate the process.

Voluntary youth organisations often rely on the LEA to help them to work together. Which may be an easy way out with regard to resources for partnership, but it can bring problems. Probably the best known example is the Bradford Metropolitan Youth and Community Consultative Committee, a well-supported coming together of the LEA's elected members and officers with representatives of the voluntary sector. It was probably the success of this committee which contributed to the Review Group on the Youth Service's decision not to be more prescriptive in recommending CVYSs as the machinery for voluntary sector co-operation in the Thompson Report[5].

The major drawback in having bodies such as Bradford's as the only machinery for the voluntary sector partnership is that they usually have to double as the forums for the voluntary/statutory partnership also. This can be unsatisfactory from the LEA's viewpoint, in that liaison with the voluntary sector means liaison with a myriad of individual representatives; and it denies the voluntary sector the separate means of arriving at a common position on any sensitive issue before they negotiate with the LEA.

Voluntary youth organisations working together in partnership with each other is one of those things, like the participation of young people, which is seen as a 'good thing', as long as it happens of its own accord. But it doesn't. Good partnership requires enabling. And whose task is it to enable voluntary youth organisations to work with each other? If it is that of the organisations themselves then, firstly, they should be aware of demands of time it will place on already busy volunteers and paid staff. Secondly, it requires those people to have the skills to facilitate partnership; of which more later. Lastly, it requires organisations to ask themselves whether there is anything in the way they operate and present themselves that may inhibit or put off potential partners.

An LEA setting out to enable the partnership between voluntary youth organisations starts with a disadvantage. Without a record of voluntary/statutory partnership within the LEA area, there may not be the required level of trust. The LEA's motives may be questioned, even if they are honourable. LEA officers wishing to promote partnership in the voluntary sector may want to consider whether it is best to establish long-term machinery, as in Bradford, which they will inevitably end up servicing, or whether a short intervention with the aim of establishing some self-sufficient machinery may not be more productive.

The Thompson Report was clear as to whose role is the enabling of the voluntary sector partnership. It stated 'In order to function effectively, a consortium (of voluntary youth organisations) will need administrative and staff support', and went on to recommend a specific appointment. Since the Report came out in 1982, an increasing number of CVYSs have appointed paid staff, usually with the help of LEA grant aid. The results, in the form of a more cohesive, better informed and better represented voluntary sector, may well persuade more LEAs that investing in such posts is worthwhile.

The voluntary/statutory partnership

The partnership between the voluntary sector and the local authority youth service has always been a difficult one. Doubtless, from the start, the established voluntary youth organisations resented the intervention of local government into a service which they had been running for decades. And, later, few of the voluntary organisations could compete with the glossy purpose-built post-Albemarle youth centres, and there must have been some envy around. Now, after years of restraint in public spending, the recent central government emphasis on the voluntary ethos may have caused the feelings to be the other way around.

Of course, both sectors would say that it really was not the way it appeared and, given the low level of the national resource which goes into the service as a whole, both may argue with justification that there never has been any basis for the jealousy. But can each make the other hear? Is there some forum for these views to be shared? Unfortunately, the answer is too often 'No'. Which may be one reason why the youth service has never been able to mount a lobby effective enough to increase its share of the national resource.

In recent years, both the Thompson Report and then the Department of Education and Science Circular 1/85[6] have laid emphasis on the need for voluntary youth organisations and local authority youth services to plan their future provision in consultation with each other, echoing the 1939 Board of Education Circular, referred to earlier.

In spite of over 40 years of exhortation, my own research in 1983[7] showed that the machinery for voluntary/statutory partnership was, at that time, meagre. Of 89 LEAs which responded to a questionnaire, about three-quarters were aware of some consortium through which the voluntary sector aimed to come together in partnership. But only 37 of the 89 gave this voluntary sector consortium any representation on either their policy-making or advisory committees for the youth service.

Douglas Smith, in his analysis of LEA policy developments following Thompson[8], published in 1987, saw some improvement in this situation. He stated 'The reaffirmation of the partnership principle was expressed clearly in the reviews in the form of ... a greater involvement and role in Youth Service decision-making'. But these improvements were starting from a low base.

The most common, but arguably least productive method of promoting the statutory/voluntary partnership, is the LEA elected member or youth officer sitting on the voluntary organisation's management committee. This is usually a condition of LEA grant aid. Although this can inform the officer, and can provide a useful forum for the giving of professional advice, it can be an uncomfortable situation. Is the officer there as an adviser, or as a watchdog over the LEA's investment? Elected members usually have so many other commitments that only rarely do they appear often enough to play an effective role. A single LEA representative may be able to convey the authority's views to the voluntary organisation but, especially if the representative is an officer, it is unlikely that this method can provide an adequate channel for the voluntary organisation's views on any LEA proposal.

The method for enacting the voluntary/statutory partnership, proposed by Thompson, and which has gained some favour with both LEAs and the voluntary sector, is the local joint youth advisory committee. This has representation from the LEA, the voluntary sector and, at least in Thompson's recommendation, young people. Its task is to advise the authority on its youth service policy and, in doing that, provide a forum whereby the voluntary sector may also consult on its own proposals.

Such advisory committees have, on the whole, proved successful. But they vary in their detail and methods, with corresponding effects on the partnership.

The advisory committee may gain its voluntary sector representation from a number of individual voluntary organisations, or from a voluntary sector consortium or CVYS. Individual representation has proven effective in some LEAs, but it necessitates either a quite large committee or, alternatively, leaving some organisations out. It means that the voluntary sector also has to enact its own internal partnership through the advisory committee, as discussed above, giving it an extra role and demanding time in the committee to achieve this purpose.

Gaining representation from a CVYS, or similar body is more convenient, as long as the CVYS involves the majority of the voluntary organisations in the area and is an effective body. If not, it can put influence into the hands of a comparatively small group of people, who may lack the machinery, ability or intention to share it. Which gives the LEA a vested interest in ensuring that there is an effective and broadly representative voluntary sector consortium.

In some LEAs the committee departs from being simply advisory, and has delegated powers from the education or leisure committee of the authority. This can cause complications, in that the legal framework within which local government operates lays down that, in principle, only elected members can decide on the spending of the authority's money. There are ways round this, but it is not clear whether or not they are worth the effort.

Delegating to a youth advisory committee the allocation of funds, such as grant aid to the voluntary sector, may be convenient for the superior committee, but it can lead to an inordinate amount of time being spent on this at the expense of more important issues about the future direction of the service. It is more advisable for the advisory committee to give its time to agreeing overall aims and guidelines for grant aid, and then ask the superior committee to decide within these parameters. In this way there is more chance of avoiding petty inter-organisation squabbles and reaching some consensus on youth service policy.

A more detailed discussion of local authority grant aid to voluntary youth organisations, and its effect on the recipients, can be found in the appendix to the Policy Studies Institute publication, *A Price Worth Paying*[9].

As discussed in the section on the partnership between voluntary youth organisations, some LEAs prefer to promote the voluntary/statutory partnership at a more local level. This is often the case where the authority operates a community education system. Some form of area youth committee, serviced by an LEA area officer and often with delegated powers over small amounts of grant aid, brings together the voluntary youth organisations, the LEA-maintained service and, sometimes, the local LEA elected member.

These area committees can provide a useful local forum, but they depend heavily on the skills of the area officer in enabling the partnership; something rarely learned in either initial or in-service training. Further, the area officer can see the area youth committee as the only task with real power attached to what is often an advisory role. The temptation to play power games is sometimes irresistible. Before establishing area youth committees, or appointing a new officer to operate within such a system, LEAs should carefully review the job description for the post and then ensure that there is a process for assessing and updating the skills required.

Area youth committees should never be seen as the sole forums for partnership between LEAs and the voluntary sector. Many voluntary youth organisations have structures which mean that local policy decisions can only be taken at a county level, or even higher. And LEA consultation with the voluntary sector should be conducted at the level at which the policy is made.

With the regional pilot projects promoted by the National Youth Bureau and the devolution of the grant-making function of the Youth Exchange Centre to the regional level, voluntary/statutory partnership at this level has assumed a new importance. Mostly, such partnership has focussed on the youth sub-committees of Regional Advisory Councils for Further Education (RACs). The nine RACs in England are the means whereby most LEAs come together to compare policy and co-operate on all aspects of FE. All but one has a sub-committee which relates to the youth service.

Since 1980, almost all the RACs have sought voluntary sector representation on their youth sub-committees. But there is a dilemma inherent in their involvement in what are essentially LEA bodies. Some principal youth officers would argue that it is their task to liaise with the voluntary sector within their LEA, and to have knowledge of its work and views. If this is so, then the principal youth officers can speak about the voluntary sector when discussing comparative policy and training needs, and the voluntary sector representative to the RAC is left without a real role.

Some RAC youth sub-committees have become effective forums for the promotion of the voluntary/statutory partnership, especially partnership in training, but the role of the voluntary sector in this setting must be resolved if further results are to be expected. Further, if the RAC wishes to involve voluntary sector policy-makers, many of whom are volunteers, then consideration must be given to important details such as holding meetings at times when volunteers can attend and the payment of travel expenses.

To conclude, the voluntary/statutory partnership has developed significantly in the 1980s. But, although there are some areas of good practice, there are still too many LEA areas where partnership is a low priority for either, or both sectors. Further work needs to be done in developing machinery for the partnership which is relevant to the LEA structure and the range of voluntary youth organisations in the particular area. The DES Experimental Projects in Mangement and Training Scheme, announced in Circular 1/85, has funded a few projects which may pioneer such work in the future.

The partnership with young people

In 1960 Albemarle[10] recommended 'Young people should be given opportunities for participation as partners in the youth service'. In 1969 *Youth and Community Work in the '70s*[11] stated 'Young adults should be involved in the running of youth and community organisations, including committees with spending powers'.

Yet by 1981 Martin Shaw of the *Young People and Decisions*[12] project was able to say 'There is very little evidence within the youth service to suggest a major shift towards improving the number of opportunities for young people to participate'.

The Thompson Report sets out quite clearly the case for the participation of young people in youth service decision-making to be an essential element of the service, and those well-rehearsed arguments will not be repeated here. Neither will this chapter dwell on the need for, or the process of the involvement of young people in decision-making about activities or the organisation of the youth club or unit. Such things should already be a part of the programme of every youth organisation or agency and, if they are not, there is plenty of material elsewhere to assist the reader. The British Youth

Council has produced a useful guide to resource material on participation[13].

Here, the focus will be the three-way partnership, the involvement of young people in youth service policy-making in partnership with the voluntary sector or the LEA, or both. Arriving at a partnership with young people at this level may require a significant degree of participation at the club or unit level, or that young people will have already gained a say in society through youth councils or similar machinery. If this is not so, effort may properly be better expended on these areas before attempting to establish a three way partnership at other levels.

For young people's participation in youth service policy-making to be effective, there will first have to be some form of base within which the young people can gain experience, and to which they can return to ground their views and experiences.

As previously stated, Thompson saw at the hub of youth service policy-making a three way committee of the LEA representatives, of the voluntary sector representatives and young people. What was not clear was how these young people should be found, who they represent, if anyone, and to whom they should be responsible.

Without machinery to support their presence on a committee, young people can be merely tokens. Of course, it is important for the providers of youth service to gain the views of young people on proposals. But it would be better to conduct market research or hold a public meeting than to choose half a dozen assorted young people and put them on a committee where they have no support or back-up networks.

One way round this is to gain representation from a network of youth councils. These rarely cover effectively as wide an area as an LEA; so more than one will be required for geographical balance. If no youth council exists, either the LEA or the voluntary sector, or both acting together could promote one. The British Youth Council has expertise in facilitating such a process.

But the hours of effort which youth workers or officers put into helping to form a youth council do not guarantee success. Young people will not join a body whose main purpose is to provide an input into the youth service's committee structures. The young people will want to address issues which are of interest to them, some of them sensitive or politically contentious. Adults in the youth service cannot set up a youth council just to meet their own needs. It has to meet the needs of young people first, or they won't give it their time.

Another means of gaining young people's representation for partnership machinery is through the membership of LEA and voluntary sector organisations and clubs. The drawbacks are that this only reaches the 'clubbable' and that, unless the clubs have already reached a reasonable level of participation, there may have to be much explanation of the nuances of youth service policy before the young people can respond in an informed manner.

There is emerging a number of self-programming young people's organisations which may be approached for representation. These are groups which young people run for themselves and are based around issues or activities of their own choice. Some, such as Young Farmers' clubs and Eighteen Plus have been around for many years. But there is evidence that International Youth Year encouraged the development of many more, or at least brought them to the fore. Young people from these self-programming groups may only represent their fellow group members, but they will be in touch with a limited network outside the established youth service, and they will have some experience of the issues involved in operating provision.

Councils for Voluntary Youth Service in Cheshire, Lancashire, Nottinghamshire and Staffordshire, among others, have experimented with promoting young people's involvement in youth service policy making through their own structures. In the long term, when voluntary youth organisations become truly participative, CVYSs will involve young people, because young people will be an integral part of the individual organisation's structures. They won't need special places on committees; they will be there as full representatives, just like anyone else. However, that day is still some way off.

The danger with young people's participation in the three way partnership through CVYSs is that it, also, can be tokenistic. Again, the support structures within the individual organisations may not be sufficiently developed to make it work. Staffordshire CVYS has tried an alternative to the simple allocation of seats on the council. It established an open forum for young people from its member organisations which ran alongside, but was linked to the CVYS. In this forum, the young people debated issues of their own choice and then had the opportunity to influence the CVYS on these. It may not be a neat, democratic solution, but such ideas are well worth trying.

To conclude, Thompson and Circular 1/85 have boosted the three way partnership at the LEA level. There are a number of LEA areas where young people are being involved in decision-making about youth service policy. Some are not being confined by the traditional 'seats on committees' approach, which suits adults, but which may not be so amenable to young people. These initiatives, however, should be seen as building on, and additional to the development of participation within the club or unit. And, whatever method of promoting the three way partnership is chosen, it must not be seen as a once and for all initiative. Every succeeding generation of young people deserves fresh consideration. It cannot be assumed that they will automatically take to the structures and practices adopted by their predecessors.

The national/local partnership

Until recently, the partnership between central and local government with regard to youth service has been a tenuous one. Central government has consistently resisted setting out clear guidelines, in the form of a legislative base, on what it expects local authorities to provide for young people. Local government has often been unwilling to co-operate with central government over the youth service. Some local education authorities responded to the Secretary of State for Education's request, in DES Circular 1/85, to tell him their plans for the youth service with terse one-page letters which made it clear that they almost saw it as being none of his business.

The introduction in 1986 of the local authority training grants scheme, commonly called GRIST, through DES Circular 6/86[14], began a change in this situation. If local authorities, and through them voluntary organisations, now want to have a share of the central fund for the in-service training of youth workers, they have to bid for it from the Secretary of State.

Similarly with the Education Support Grant scheme, whereby the Secretary of State invites bids from LEAs for monies to fund educational projects, including youth service ones.

Both these schemes give central government machinery whereby it can influence directly some of the youth work undertaken by local authorities and voluntary organisations; which may be seen as a rather one-sided partnership. It will be interesting to watch out for how this national/local partnership might develop.

Inter-agency co-operation

The track record of the youth service for co-operating with other agencies working with young people is, on the whole, a poor one. Perhaps this is not surprising. The lead has been established by central government for many years. Despite numerous calls to do so, the government has repeatedly declined to establish a ministry for youth, or appoint a true minister for youth. So the various services to young people which government oversees to go without any specific co-ordination.

At a more local level, the youth service suffers from the actual process which most LEAs adopt for co-ordinating their policy. In a typical local authority, whereas the directors of education and social services will be members of a corporate planning team, the principal youth officer will have to rely on the service's message being relayed up through an assistant education officer, to the director and then back down again.

Two initiatives in this area are worthy of note. Firstly, in Wolverhampton, following a major research programme[15], the authority has established a Youth Affairs Unit which has the remit of co-ordinating the policy of all the departments of the authority with regard to young people, not just the youth service. This unit is linked to the Policy and Resources Committee of the authority, and so it is in a central position from which to influence the policy and practice of all the departments. On the other hand, being placed structurally as an adjunct to the Chief executive's department, and therefore outside any of the large well resourced departments, may leave the unit without enough muscle to carry its ideas through; the situation in which some of the similarly placed units promoting policy co-ordination with regard to black and other ethnic minority groups have found themselves.

The other initiative is the promotion of Juvenile Liaison Bureaux, where the youth service joins with the education service, the probation service, social workers and the police in an attempt to meet the needs of young offenders in the community. Northamptonshire County Council has been in the forefront of this work[16]. Juvenile Liaison Bureaux are a practical attempt at the co-ordination of policy and practice with regard to a specific area of work. It ought to be possible to extend this approach to other areas, such as a co-ordinated approach to the needs of homeless young people, for example. The method has been pioneered and could be extended elsewhere.

Co-ordination in the voluntary sector has suffered from a lack of mutual knowledge between the social welfare and community organisations, which form the bulk of the membership of Councils for Voluntary Service, and the voluntary youth organisations. This was brought home to me some years ago when, on moving to a new city, the local CVS Volunteer Bureau could not offer a single opportunity for voluntary work with a youth organisation. The voluntary youth organisations had not offered the information; and the Bureau had not asked.

Increasingly, voluntary organisations with a social welfare base are finding the situation of young people of concern to them. The links are there for the making. Local consortia for voluntary youth organisations, CVYSs or their equivalent, ought to be able to develop some means of co-ordinating their work with Councils for Voluntary Service; for example, the exchange of nominees to each other's Executive Committees. The bringing to light of opportunities for co-operation would surely follow.

At the neighbourhood level, in spite of the 'community' emphasis in youth work following the publication of *Youth and Community Work in the '70s*[11], the youth service is rarely the initiator of a co-ordinated approach. The introduction of the 'patch' system in some social service departments has meant that social workers now have an interest in local co-operation. And the return of the beat bobby through community policing also provides another, easily identifiable prospective partner. At the very least, it would be worth the youth worker inviting all the other workers with an interest in young people in the neighbourhood to an informal meeting over a sandwich lunch to discuss the scope for co-operation. It may be that from such small initiatives larger scale inter-agency co-operation may grow.

Partnership and people

Until now, this chapter has tended to discuss partnership in terms of organisations and structures. This is how the subject is usually addressed in current reports and policy documents. But the practice of partnership is an intensely personal thing. It means making time to go out of one's way to co-operate with others and, in doing so, being prepared to compromise over the way things are done.

There is a commonly held view that working in partnership is a natural thing. All that has to be done is to put people in the same room, give them an issue held in common, and they will co-operate. That isn't so. Whether it is an inherent human weakness or something taught by our society, I do not know, but in that situation people do not work together, they compete.

For partnership and participation to succeed as ways of working in the youth service requires two things.

Firstly, someone must facilitate the partnership. Someone must have the skills to recognise the potential for co-operation, and also have the resources, time and ability to promote the circumstances whereby that potential can develop.

Secondly, the people brought together by the facilitator of the partnership must have attitudes which do not reject the concept of partnership outright, and attitudes which do not prejudge potential partners as unworthy, or incapable of co-operation. They must be in a position where they feel secure enough to enter into partnerships. And they must possess the skills to work in partnership.

These pre-requisites for partnership show clearly that it is an area which requires as much effort, resource and planning as any other in youth service.

The task of facilitating partnership is one which could fall to almost anyone. Certainly, it would appear to be a key task in the job description of any LEA area or principal youth officer, as well as that of any voluntary sector regional officer and many county level officers, paid or voluntary. On the whole the skills required, those of planned intervention, negotiating and enabling, are not far removed from youth work skills, but they are worthy of specific further training. Most usefully this could be provided at the point where the youth worker assumes responsibility for work at more than unit level.

The provision of resources for partnership have, in the past, been meagre. LEAs often confuse resources for the promotion of partnership with grant aid to the voluntary sector. Few have continued the experiments into the promotion of young people's participation in youth service policy-making at anything like the same level as in International Youth Year. The voluntary sector is inclined towards seeing resources devoted to partnership more as a way of gaining greater grant aid than as their contribution to a better way of working. Resources devoted to partnership work have to be seen as a long term investment in the development of the service.

With regard to attitudes towards potential partners, the problem is that people are often unaware of their own ill-informed prejudice. As part of a recent training event, senior voluntary sector officers told each other a few key pieces of information about their own organisations. The level of misinformation and myth which this short exercise dispelled was quite high. If people knew more about each other's work, preferably learning this directly from each other, the attitudes held about potential partners in the youth service would improve enormously. Youth organisations, clubs and units would gain from assessing what it is that they have to offer to potential partners in the youth service, and what they would wish to gain from a partnership. Too often, youth workers perpetuate their organisation's public relations image, portraying it as totally self-sufficient. Which does not encourage potential partners.

Attitudes towards partnership are more difficult to deal with. We live in a society which tends to reward those people who have the strength of character to dominate, rather than those who are prepared to see and to accommodate the views and feelings of the other person. It is, therefore, not surprising that people tend to hold hostile attitudes towards co-operative working. But, if the youth service is to become truly participative, these attitudes have to be acknowledged and changed. Racism, sexism and paternalism all stem from the predisposition to devalue the other person. The youth service has to find ways of demonstrating its opposition to these ills in the way it organises and manages its work, as well as in its programmes. Learning to deal with our own attitudes towards working together would be a step in this direction.

Lack of security is a significant factor in the breakdown of partnerhip. To work in partnership requires negotiation. If youth workers or officers do not know whether or not they have the power to negotiate on an issue, then they will feel insecure. Similarly with the three way partnership, the youth council which makes demands which have a potential for embarrassing the youth officer with elected members is not going to get support, unless the officer is secure within some agreed policy framework for this work. There is a danger that the person attempting participative or co-operating working can be left, like piggy in the middle – having raised expectation in potential partners, but then finding that the power to fulfill those expectations is not available.

Lastly, all middle managers in youth service – that is those with any managerial function at all – need in-service training in the skills required for partnership work. Only when a youth officer addressing a new issue is able to say, not 'What can I and my organisation do about this?', but 'What can I and my organisation enable the youth service as a whole, including young people, to do about this?', will the youth service partnership have become established.

References

1. Department of Education and Science (1939), *Circular 1486*, HMSO.
2. (1986) *Fair Shares?* Liverpool Council for Voluntary Service.
3. Green, C (1986) *In the Service of Youth*, National Council for Voluntary Youth Services, p. 6.
4. Garrett, B (1986) *1,000 Links: Youth Activity in Croydon*, Croydon Guild of Voluntary Organisations.
5. The Thompson Report (1982), *Experience and Participation: Report of the Review Group on the Youth Service in England*, Command 8686, HMSO.
6. Department of Education and Science (1985), *Circular 1/85*, HMSO.
7. Smith, D R (1983), *Partnership in the Youth Service*, National Council for Voluntary Youth Services.
8. Smith, D I (1987) *Reshaping the Youth Service*, National Youth Bureau, p. 12.
9. Leat, D (1986), *A Price Worth Paying?*, Policy Studies Institute.
10. (1959) *The Youth Service in England and Wales*, HMSO.
11. Youth Service Development Council (1969), *Youth and Community Work in the '70s*, HMSO.

12. Foster, A and Shaw, M (1981), *Young People and Decisions*, National Council for Voluntary Youth Services.
13. Joseph, S (1984), *Youth Participation into Practice*, British Youth Council.
14. Department of Education and Science (1986), *Circular 6/86*, HMSO.
15. Willis, P (1985), *The Social Condition of Young People in Wolverhampton*, Wolverhampton Borough Council.
16. (1984) *Diversion – Corporate Action With Juveniles*, Northamptonshire County Council.

8 Resources and financial management

Chris Tomsett

For the purposes of this chapter, resources have been identified simply as money; money that can then be used in the acquisition, maintenance and development of people, buildings, things and programmes. Given this definition it is accepted that 'financial management' is inextricably linked both with the attainment and deployment of resources. Indeed, the ability to demonstrate 'good housekeeping' may be a prerequisite of any successful application for additional resources.

To assist both the writer and the reader, however, the two issues are dealt with in separate sections. It is assumed that their interdependence will be borne in mind throughout.

Resources

Choosing an analogy to introduce this section on resources for the youth service proved difficult. On the one hand it needed to show the positive side of a multi-faceted, open-ended range of resourcing; on the other lack of clarity and preciseness as to what exactly youth service resources are.

In 'Alice in Wonderland', Alice had a conversation with the Cheshire Cat that went:

Alice: 'Which way should I go?'
Cheshire Cat: 'That depends where you want to get to.'
Alice: 'I don't much mind, as long as I get somewhere.'
Cheshire Cat: 'Then it doesn't matter which direction you go – so long as you go far enough!'

Aspects of the Alice problem are sometimes found by those seeking resources in the youth service. It is not, however, the destination that causes the uncertainty, rather the means of travel, and possibly the route. For most resource seekers the answer would be similar: as long as you can go far enough you will find the resources that you need.

The youth service is an umbrella title used for many practices. Within England and Wales alone there are 109 local education authorities, each making some form of youth service provision which may or may not be similar. Each of these will have a different selection of the range of voluntary organisations operating within their boundaries. NCVYS has in membership some 80 organisations and in addition to these is a wide spectrum of organisations that includes music and drama groups, hobbies and sports clubs, international and political groups that are involved in the social education of young people. Those working within the service will be quick to realise that this diversity is not the unique property of the youth service: the diversity also exists in the range of sources of funding. Therefore a word of caution is necessary: within these pages it is only possible to present a range of examples and issues related to the problem of acquiring resources. This does not pretend to be a definitive document. Here are given some examples of national, regional and local funding initiatives that are most likely to be duplicated elsewhere; we point the direction for those seeking more information on new and different funding sources. Issues about the process of seeking resources that are transferable from situation to situation are not raised.

Background: a national perspective

During the 1980's there has been an increasing recognition of the complex and confused nature of resources and funding within the youth service. This is perhaps best summarised by quoting from the introductory section of *Expenditure on the Youth Service – 1978-83*[1]:

> In recent years there has been a growing interest and concern both about the resources available to the youth service and about the accuracy and scope of our knowledge of them. The Thompson Report contained much useful information but was itself hampered by the lack of data about the Youth Service provision.
>
> It should be said at the outset that the creation of a picture of expenditure on the youth service is difficult to achieve for a number of reasons:
>
> ... confusion or uncertainty about the exact meaning of the figures derived from central government sources.
>
> ... at least one major change in the basis on which the actual expenditure figures for the youth service were published.

... the complete absence of any standard procedure by which local authorities themselves allocate and record expenditure on youth service.

Further complications have arisen in recent years with the growth of funding from non-traditional sources. In one form or another the MSC has become a major financial supporter of some forms of youth provision.

Finally, the highly variable location and structure of the youth service in different local authorities adds further uncertainty to the meaning of the published expenditure figures. Some authorities have located the youth service in non-education departments, e.g. leisure and recreation, yet financial returns for some of these appear within education statistics. Additionally, authorities have adopted different structures for the service, with some placing a relatively high priority and allocating a relatively high proportion of resources to the voluntary sector whilst others have concentrated on direct local authority provision.

Seeking resources: the process

Why seek resources? This may be seen as an unnecessary and naïve question. Not so: if any organisation is to pursue the acquisition of funds from an external source it needs to be able to answer coherently and precisely a number of seemingly obvious questions:

- Why are more resources needed?
- Is the project/organisation to be funded worthwhile?
- Is it more worthwhile than that which is being done at the moment? Should existing funds be diverted?
- Are the objectives firmly located within the wider plan?
- Are the objectives clearly within the responsibilities and interests of the funding agency we have identified?

Those working with young people today do so in a society that has changed and is changing rapidly. Many of the hallmarks that stamped the path from childhood to adulthood no longer exist: a state of flux is dominant. This creates a situation in which agencies and organisations are frequently having to review and change their style of operation. Very few organisations operate with infinite resources: the changes demanded increase the pressure on funds, and increase the pressure for clear identification and prioritisation of objectives.

Clear objectives are not only essential for the good management of existing resources; they are a pre-requisite for the acquisition of funds from other sources. To convince other people that they should give their money you must be clear about why it is needed, what it will achieve, and how its use and usefulness will be monitored and evaluated.

There are certain ground rules that need to be followed in the pursuit of funds. The precise way in which an application has to be made will vary from funding body to funding body. The preparation of the applicant needs to be basically the same; the elements she/he needs to demonstrate are diagramatically represented in Figure 8.1 (below). In operational practice this becomes a cyclical model, with a further link being made: the evaluation leads directly to a revision of the need/objective, and the process starts again.

Consideration must be given as to who makes the application for funding. There are some resourcing agencies that will assist in the funding of youth work initiatives irrespective of whether they are located within the statutory or the voluntary sector. There are others that will only assist in the funding of voluntary projects and organisations. It must be remembered that there are many voluntary organisations in existence, particularly at local level that were established to meet specific needs, and to gain access to sources of funding that would not otherwise have been available. Not only does this, on occasions, make sound financial sense – it also can be a vital

Figure 8.1

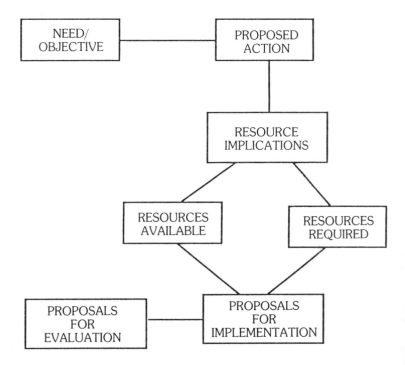

element of community development, in enabling local people to play a direct role.

Most youth services have a tiered structure, such as the model shown in Figure 8.2. It is essential to recognise that outside funding may be available in different forms, for different ends, at each level.

Sources of funding: some examples

Local authorities

In most areas the local education authority is a major provider of funds for the youth service – both in the form of direct provision through the statutory service, and in the disbursement of funds (or similar) to voluntary organisations, often to all three levels of the model shown in Figure 8.2.

A breakdown of the areas in which LEAs provide funding would include:

- Youth work buildings
- Full time staffing
- Part time staffing

Figure 8.2

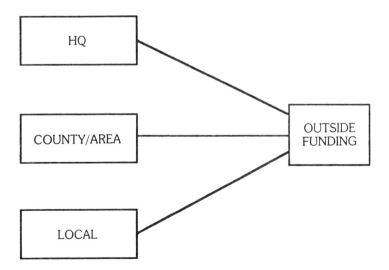

- Staff development/training
- Access to premises
- Accommodation/rent support
- Experimental projects
- Equipment purchase

The three tier model applied to a voluntary organisation within one rural area may, for example, be able to obtain support from the LEA in three ways:

- Grant towards HQ staff
- Staff development programmes at an area level
- Grant towards rental of premises at a local level

There is a growing emphasis within local authorities on inter-departmental, inter-agency initiatives. This reflects the call in the Thompson Report for greater co-operation between those departments concerned with the affairs of young people. The implication for those seeking resouces is that funding for work with young people may not be restricted just to the youth service. Some examples from one county authority would include:

- Volunteer training (education/social services)
- Crime prevention panel (education/social services/police)
- Drugs education programmes (health/social services/education/police)
- Holiday schemes (social services/education)
- Rural information service (libraries/education)

The other tiers of local authorities may not have a direct statutory responsibility for the youth service, but should not be ignored as possible funding sources. District councils, town and parish councils are all bodies that can be persuaded, at an area and local level, that a caring authority should be giving support to projects designed to enhance the life of its citizens. Appropriate parallels to the following examples are identifiable in most local situations:

Town/parish funding obtained for:
- International projects
- Playschemes
- Youth action schemes
- Newsletter
- Equipment
District council:
- Outreach work on DC estate
- International project
- Drugs advice initiative
- Equipment.

Local bodies

The importance of very local resourcing bodies must not be ignored, although they are too numerous to list in detail. The sums of money may in themselves be small: in total, and in their importance to the recipient organisations, they are substantial. The range of such bodies varies from area to area, but anywhere in the country there are groups similar to Rotary Clubs, Round Table and Gala Committees, etc.

Trust funds – regional and national bodies

There is neither space nor time to list the trust funds that are available and willing to consider resourcing organisations and projects related to the needs of young people. A comprehensive source of information is the *Director of Grant-Making Trusts*[2], produced by Charities Aid Foundation (available in most local libraries). It is appropriate to make particular mention here of the Royal Jubilee Trusts:

> King George's Jubilee Trust – founded 1935 to assist the physical mental and spiritual development of young people, to provide financial support for voluntary youth projects in specific areas of priority.

> Princes Trust – founded 1976 to help disadvantaged young people help themselves, to provide small, one-off grants to young people who produce their own proposals aimed at establishing self-help projects.

> The Queens Silver Jubilee Trust – established 1977, principally to help young people help others of any age in the community, and to put resources directly in the hands of young volunteers.

The Sports Council and Arts Council are two national bodies with a clearly identifiable regional structure. Both of these organisations, in their respective field of operation, have given much support at all levels to those working with young people. Contact information is given in the reference list, and discussions with regional officers would identify the particular area of interest which may be common. Recent examples include:

- Part-funding towards upgrading of outside play area
- Development of sports centres in rural areas
- Travel assistance in rural areas
- Staff training in the use of video with young people
- Assistance with creation of youth film crew
- Appointment of part-time worker in creative arts

The scope is endless: particular projects may well have particular sources of funding – art work, international work, health education, conservation and environmental issues. Lack of funds need not, in the first instance, be a reason for not pursuing an idea for the resolution of a need. If the priority is high, then the allocation of time needs to be made to ensure that someone within the organisation can explore the myriad funding opportunities that exist. Seeking the source and preparing the case will be time consuming but if the objectives have been correctly prioritised then it is indeed justifiable use of time.

Financial management

There is a continual tension that exists over the use of resources – a tension between their use for maintenance of programmes, or the development of programmes. Once a programme has been established there is often an inbuilt expectation that the level of resourcing will be maintained, or even grow. Once a post has been established it will be seen as permanent. In the world of infinite resources this would not be a problem: given the finite nature of the funding that most youth service personnel have available, it causes tension. Commenting on the role of the local authority officer in relation to the youth service, Professor John Eggleston said in the mid 1970's, that often the policy pursued was a 'policy for containment in which organisations received for established and recognised activities, and only infrequently succeeded in making the case for new ones'. This attitude is no longer paramount, though one needs to be constantly on guard about falling into the trap.

To paraphrase Edmund Burke, a youth service without the means of change is without the means of its own conservation. The last decade has seen phenomenal change in society, and reference has already been made to the impact of change on young people. Youth service 'providers', voluntary and statutory, are faced increasingly with the need to constantly change and develop styles of work. This in turn necessitates an approach to financial management that is enabling and flexible, rather than restrictive and rigid.

The paragraphs that follow are not intended to provide textbook information on accounting procedures, systems, etc. They are an attempt to point out some of the choices and issues confronting those responsible for the financial resources of the youth service: the managers of money. Very few people are in a position to establish a completely new system of financial management. Most managers within the youth service will be operating in a wider structure that will require conformity to established systems. Whilst it may be possible to negotiate for change over a period of time, the requirements of a given system will have to be met. The skill for the manager will lie in the creative exploitation of the system.

Financial management is but one aspect of management. Whilst it relates to a particular function it also crosses all the boundaries of the management function. To a large extent, therefore, the style chosen for the financial management will be related to the style chosen for the overall management function. It can be argued that the general principles of management must ensure that:

- The service is effective
- Potential is recognised and developed
- The ability to change and grow is inherent.

All these principles also relate to financial management – and in financial terms all have to be done at the same time, they are not three different tasks. The future shape of the service is not going to be made tomorrow: it is being made today, and largely by the decisions and actions taken with regard to the tasks of today. Conversely, what is being done to bring about the future directly affects the present. The tasks overlap and they require a unified strategy of financial management. The model in Figure 8.3 is simply an expanded, more representative version of the one presented earlier. It can be taken to generally represent the structure of either a statutory or a voluntary service; it can be located at any level – HQ could be national, regional, county or town; it can relate to an organisation based or project based system. It is recognised that it is a simplification – the model may well be located within a larger, highly complex structure. A manager at HQ level may well have accountabilities 'upwards'. The principles that can be applied to this model, however, are to a large extent transferable to other situations.

The organisation represented in the structure will need to formulate decisions, and determine actions around three areas:

Figure 8.3 – Location of resource control

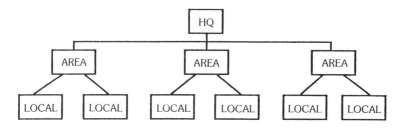

- The identification of objectives
- The acquisition and allocation of funds
- Delivery styles – the functional level.

Within each of these areas there is a choice: the choice also applies to finance. One can opt for a system where the control of finances is located with just a few people, or one can opt for a more open system where power is more widely diffused. The difficulty, and therefore the skill, lies in striking an appropriate balance between a tight, personal control of resources and the creation of sufficient space and confidence to allow innovation and growth. This is a political decision in the best sense of the word: it is about one's perception of the use of power, of one's view of staff development, and one's willingness to demonstrate a faith in the competence of other people. The differing scope of control is represented in Figure 8.4. The more open a system can become, the closer to the point of use that decisions can be made about finances, the more responsive a structure can become to the changing needs of young people within the community.

Monitoring

The corollary is that the more open the system, the more sophisticated the monitoring and evaluation needs to be. Accountability must be inescapable, whatever the system. The responsiblity for financial performance at all levels must be capable of allocation to individuals. A regular pattern of monitoring must then be established and its understanding ensured.

Once again the financial tasks cannot truly be separated from the wider management function. It is true that it is essential to establish systems of financial monitoring – the submission of accounts, regular

Figure 8.4

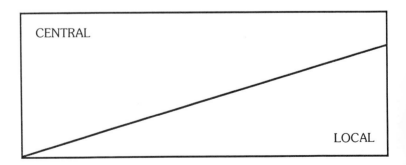

and full auditing procedures, forecasts, computerised and manual systems of recording. These will lead to a breakdown of costs on areas such as personnel, buildings, equipment. These can be balanced against income, users etc. Good systems will produce sound financial information on quantifiable phenomena. It cannot show the unquantifiable – either the personal growth and development that is often the outcome of a youth work initiative, or what an agency has chosen not to do. A full evaluation needs to extend across the full management function. To move from today to tomorrow, the financial manager needs to look just as closely at the wider demands of the service as at the latest computer print-out, or annual balance sheet. In a paper, 'Performance Indicators in the Education Service'[3], it was noted that '... there is a wide range of purposes, only some of which lend themselves to measurement. No one indicator is enough. There must be a set. The indicators as a set only start to be useful when they provoke sensible questions in a general context'.

Budget preparation
Any well-run organisation needs to prepare budgets, to forecast the financial requirements that are necessary if it is to achieve its objectives. Two approaches are suggested below for consideration.

1. The traditional approach
The traditional approach, certainly within the statutory sector, has been to determine the appropriate level of the next year's funding from the expenditure base within the current year. In a period of no-growth this may not have been a particularly bad thing, and indeed if the initial allocation of costings was done accurately and imaginatively it may present no real problems. It can, however, be restrictive, and produce two unhelpful side effects.

The first of these is the avoidance of the sin of under-spending. The visual presentation of what this often means is shown in Figure 8.5.

Given the nature of the system it is obviously better to ensure that the money is spent by the end of the year. But can the pattern in 8.5 really be the most sensible way of allocating the resources? Some enhanced spending in month 12 possibly cannot be avoided, because of contingency sums that one will hold. Careful planning, however, should safeguard against this extreme effect.

The second side effect of this form of budgeting is its tendency to sustain the status quo. The drive to ensure the maintenance of budgets against all odds appears to be inbuilt into managers. Whilst an admirable end in itself, it can mean that one argues strongly for a particular budget allocation that could be used more imaginatively

Figure 8.5

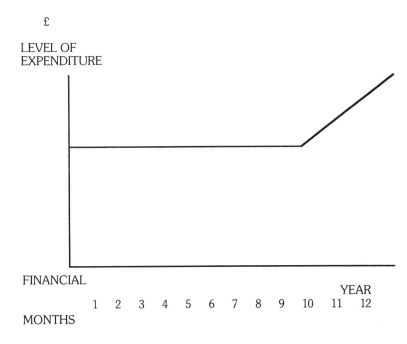

£

LEVEL OF
EXPENDITURE

FINANCIAL
                                                                        YEAR
          1   2   3   4   5   6   7   8   9   10   11   12
MONTHS

elsewhere. It partly depends on the extent to which global or specific sums are considered in the budget build-up.

2. Zero base budgeting
A different approach is contained in the theory and practice of zero base budgeting. Put at its simplest, the approach is to stop the world and start again, but in practice it needs to operate slightly differently. The principles are straightforward:

(a) do not start from current levels of expenditure;
(b) focus on the activities identified as the means of achieving the objectives;
(c) identify the essential cost requirements.

It must be noted that an assumption is made in (b) that specific organisation objectives have been determined at all of the three levels of the model presented earlier).

Allocations can then be made on the basis of (c), the essential cost requirements, taking account two other factors:

- The minimum level required to maintain viability of an organisation or project
- The incremental level required if it is to achieve additional or changed objectives, or respond to changed demands.

In practice it may be advantageous to use both systems as part of a package. If applied effectively it seems highly unlikely that it will be necessary to revert to the first principles of zero base budgeting every year. Therefore, it may be appropriate to engage in this process at specified intervals – say, three or five years. In the intervening years the allocation could be successfully adjusted, based on the year performance.

The political dimension of budgeting must not be ignored. Whatever system is employed, it is most likely that senior managers will need to argue for more resources, either from within the system, or from outside. One needs to consider the basis on which such arguments can be built: the overall inclinations of the elected members or the members of the management board; the relationship to other possible developments within the organisation; have they established priorities on a wider front that can be usefully exploited? Who are the key figures to brief? What support information will be needed? Should the case concentrate on finance, or on the social educational benefits to young people? The analysis undertaken in the course of the budget preparation must also be one that can be used to inform the political process.

Conclusion

The interdependency of the two aspects of this chapter – resources and financial management – was clearly stressed at the outset. The initial picture that was drawn indicated a broad base of funding possibilities, partly as a result of history, partly to do with broad range of interests and forms inherent within the youth service. To gain access to additional funds, and to manage new and existing resources in an effect it has been argued that it is essential to:

- Plan, prioritise, establish clear objectives
- Develop systems of monitoring and evaluation
- Identify the most appropriate level of decision making
- Ensure constant appraisal of the use and allocation of all resources
- Remember the context – the political dimension.

There is one final aspect of the use of resources and financial management that must be mentioned. The link between these has long been recognised: turn to Matthew 25 and read the parable of the talents. The rewards went to those who took justifiable risks. Creative use of resources does bring with it the necessity of occasionally taking risks. Of these there are essentially four kinds: the risk that is inherent in the everyday operation of the organisation; the risk that one can afford to take; the risk that one cannot afford to take; the risk that one cannot afford not to take.

Financial managers need to take cognisance of all the information received through all their other management functions in identifying the category of the risk facing them, as they search for the best means of ensuring that the service they manage is constantly seeking to realise the talents and energies of young people.

References

1.   Smith, D (1984), *Expenditure on the Youth Service – 1978–83*, National Youth Bureau.
2.   (1986), *Directory of Grant Making Trusts* Charities Aid Foundation.
3.   (1986), *'Performance Indicators in the Education Service'*, Chartered Institute of Public Finance Accounting.

9 Management of projects funded through specific programmes

Roger Casemore

Introduction

I remember as a young teenager being soundly reprimanded by my parents because I was unable to save anything from my pocket money. They told me that I let money burn a hole in my pocket. It seemed to me that as soon as I got it, money demanded to be spent and was therefore usually used on passing pleasures. In recent years it has struck me that this could also be a description of a management approach to money obtained via central government for spending on specific programmes. 'Hot money' seems an apt description of such funds and 'How to handle hot money' is probably the best way of describing the theme of this chapter.

I will try to identify some of the management issues and concerns arising from specific programme funds and the ways in which these impinge on the youth service manager using them to extend and develop new provision for young people. In addition to the guidelines provided by the relevant funding government departments and agencies, most local authorities will have their own internal guidelines and procedures, which may vary considerably but will all provide clear descriptions of the funds available, the criteria for application and the procedures for submission. It is important to note that the details of these guidelines and procedures and their applicability, are subject to frequent change. I will not, therefore, attempt to deal in detail with those aspects of specific programme funding. In any case, *Government Grants*[1] an NCVO practical guide already fills that role more than adequately.

Instead I will focus on some of the management and decision-making processes involved, some of the constraints surrounding the management of projects funded by these measures and some of the internal and external politics arising from them.

Specific programmes

The particular programmes to which I am referring are those concerned with issues which central government has identified as being particularly problematic and in need of special measures to respond to them. These issues include unemployment, young people at risk and in trouble, particular educational curriculum problems, and the cultural and language needs of ethnic minorities. The specific programmes include; Urban Programme schemes, Community Programme schemes, Education Support Grants, DES experimental projects and Section 11 funding. All of these have been established by central government to encourage local authorities and voluntary organisations to develop special measures for responding to different social and educational issues at a local level. A basic principle of most of these schemes is that the local authority often has to provide matching funding from within its own existing resources.

At this point it may be helpful to outline some of the most commonly used and perhaps most problematic specific programmes.

Section 11 funding

As from October 1986, the Home Office has established revised criteria for Section 11 funding. Under Section 11 of the 1966 Local Government Act, grants are payable to local authorities to enable them to employ additional staff in areas where there are 'substantial numbers of Commonwealth immigrants'. These grants can only be used for 75 per cent of the approved staffing costs of salaries and national insurance and superannuation. The other 25 per cent of the staffing costs and all other resource implications must be met by the local authority from within its existing budget. In order to be considered for a grant, the following criteria must be met:

i) The post must be designed to meet the special needs of people of Commonwealth origin, particularly in relation to language.

ii) The submission must be supported by an analysis of identified needs.

iii) The post must clearly represent special provision.

iv) In describing the post, clear objectives must be identified along with measurable performance indicators and an evaluation procedure.

v) A clearly identified consultation procedure must have taken place with the intending beneficiaries.

vi) The name and working location of the post holder when appointed must be readily available.

Education support grants

The Education (Grants and Awards) Act 1984 empowers the Secretary of State for Education and Science to pay education support grants to local education authorities in England and Wales. The aim of education support grants as stated in DES Circular 5/86 is:

> . . . to encourage local education authorities to redeploy a limited amount of expenditure into activities which appear to the Secretary of State to be of particular importance. They are intended to promote continuing improvements in the education service and to assist local education authorities to respond to changing demands. The grants are not designed to lead to an increase in aggregate local authority expenditure.

Grants are normally awarded for the one year only and grants towards expenditure in succeeding years are dependent partly on the willingness of the Secretary of State to continue funding those projects, partly on the progress of the projects and partly on the total amounts of ESG money available related to the emergence of new demands and priorities. Such grants will only cover 70 per cent of total approved expenditure of a scheme, the local authority having to provide the other 30 per cent from within existing resources.

At the present time, there are five categories under which education support grants are available to the youth service:

i) A pilot project devised to meet the needs of persons from ethnic minorities, to promote harmony between racial groups or in other ways to prepare persons for life in a multi-ethnic society.

ii) A pilot project devised to promote social responsibility in children and young people.

iii) The planning, development and coordination of provision to meet the educational needs (including the need for guidance) of persons who are unemployed (excluding those currently receiving full-time education).

iv) Where provision to meet the need of the unemployed for
educational guidance is being planned, developed and co-
ordinated, the planning, development and coordination of such
guidance for other adult persons.
v) Combatting, through education, the misuse of drugs.

These grants are not available equally to all local authorities and
considerable effort has to be put into preparing a competitive
submission in order to achieve approval of a grant.

Urban Programme schemes

The Urban Programme was established by the Local Government
Grants (Social Need) Act 1969 to make money available for use by
local authorities and through them to voluntary organisations in
urban areas. The programme is focussed on providing funds for a
range of economic, social, cultural and environmental projects with
an emphasis on promoting the economic regeneration of urban
areas.

The grants are made available for renewable periods of four or five
years to cover both capital and revenue costs. In each case, the
Department of the Environment pays up to 75 per cent of the total
cost and the local authority the remaining 25 per cent both for its own
projects and those of local voluntary organisations.

In August 1986, the Department of the Environment announced
major changes to simplify the Urban Programme, which took effect
in March 1987. Funding is now available to local authorities which
have been given 'Inner Area' status. These authorities are divided
into seven 'Inner City Partnerships' and 47 Inner Area Programmes.
The key feature of the revised Urban Programme scheme is the
requirement that both partnership and programme authorities must
produce a coordinated strategic plan for tackling their urban
problem in consultation with voluntary organisations and the
business sector.

Community Programme schemes

This is one of several strategies funded by the Manpower Services
Commission aimed at the long term unemployed and was introduced
in 1982 to replace the Community Enterprise Programme. The aim
of the scheme is to provide 245,000 temporary jobs for unemployed
adults on work which benefits the community and would not
otherwise be done. The jobs can be either full- or part-time and may
last for up to one year. Union agreement must be obtained for any
project and the agreed rate for the job must be paid to employees.

Since the MSC will only pay average wage costs of £67 per person this means that more than 75 per cent of the jobs are part-time as few sponsors are in a position to top up wages from their existing resources.

The Community Programme is supposedly open to all age groups, specifically for the long term unemployed. Applicants aged over 25 must have been unemployed for 12 of the previous 15 months, and those aged between 18 and 24 for six of the previous nine months. Married women are only eligible to participate in the scheme if their husbands are receiving unemployment benefit.

Any organisation or individual may sponsor a project, except political organisations which are specifically barred from doing so. Sponsors are expected to have the necessary management skills to operate a project and access to sufficient financial resources to provide for expenses not covered by the MSC grant.

The MSC will pay for:

(a) full time wage costs at the agreed local rate for the job of supervisors and managers of a scheme including employers' National Insurance contributions;

(b) the cost of wages for workers on the scheme up to a maximum of £67 per week. Individual workers may receive more than £67 in wages so long as the average wage across a project does not exceed this figure;

(c) the MSC will also refund operating costs such as essential overheads, materials and equipment up to a maximum of £440 per year for each individual employed on the scheme;

(d) up to a maximum of £10 per week from the wages element of the total grant may be used to organise training for employees provided it is related to the work of the project and will improve the individual's prospects of getting a permanent job;

(e) as many projects will be relatively small, employers can opt to become managing agents running a number of projects. Managing agents receive a supplementary fee of £100 per year for each Community Programme place for which they are responsible.

Young people's eligibility for the Community Programme has changed with the introduction of the new Job Training Scheme (JTS), in 1987. This is aimed specifically at 18 to 25 year-olds unemployed for longer than six months. Government clearly intends that JTS will be the preferred scheme for this age group and therefore the Community Programme will be the preferred scheme for those over 25.

Within the Community Programme there are two schemes[2] which are particularly aimed at developing further opportunities for voluntary service by unemployed people, in which they may participate without any effect on their unemployment benefits. These are:

(a) The Voluntary Projects Programme (VPP): aims to provide unemployed people with a constructive activity which might develop their existing skills or provide some form of part time rehabilitation or preparation for returning to work. Two types of project are supported by the MSC: volunteer community work and education training projects. The focus of VPP schemes is clearly an employment related objective to demonstrate that the involvement of unemployed people in VPP activities directly increases their employability;

(b) Opportunities for Volunteering (OFV) aims to develop opportunities for unemployed people to undertake voluntary work, to expand voluntary action in the fields of health and personal social services and to spend money so that, as far as possible, long term benefit to the community is obtained. The priorities of OFV are, therefore, more clearly concerned with service delivery than with employability.

Grant related in-service training (GRIST)

In 1986 the Secretary of State for Education and Science published DES Circular 6/86[3], giving details of the new arrangements for in-service training grants to local education authorities. This new scheme replaced the local authority pooling arrangements for in-service training and for TRIST – ie training related to the Technical Vocational Education Initiative (TVEI). GRIST is intended to improve the quality of teaching and to further the professional development of teachers and others in specified related fields, including youth and community work.

General principles of the scheme are: to promote the professional development of teachers and others; to promote more systematic and purposeful planning of in-service training; to encourage more effective management of teachers; and to focus training on selected areas, which are accorded national priority.

Local authorities can apply for grants under two categories. The first is in relation to training in certain selected national priority areas, for which a grant of 70 per cent will be payable. The second is in relation to training provided in response to locally assessed needs and priorities, for which a grant of 50 per cent will be payable. Each authority is allocated a grant for training for locally assessed priorities and separate grants for each national training area. The scheme applies to:

i) the further training as teachers, of qualified teachers, whether or not they are currently employed as such;

ii) the initial or further training of unqualified teachers;

iii) the training of qualified teachers as: (a) youth and community workers, (b) educational psychologists, (c) education inspectors or advisers.

iv) The initial or further training of youth and community workers (defined as

any person in any category of employment connected with leisure time facilities of a kind which local authorities have a duty to provide under sections 41(5) and 53(1) of the 1944 Education Act except those employed in solely administrative, secretarial, clerical or management capacity),

working to discharge a statutory function of an education authority.

Authorities may therefore apply for grants for training of those in this category who are employed by voluntary organisations.

Training which is eligible for grants may include any activity which will contribute to improving the development, expertise or effectiveness of the specified types of trainees. It may include school or college based training, training courses, secondments to industry and commerce and secondments of trainers to schools.

Expenditure eligible for reimbursement through grant aid includes:

i) Tuition, examination fees, residential and other charges.

ii) Travelling, subsistence and other incidental expenses of trainees.

iii) Remuneration of employees required to take the place of trainees released for training.

iv) Costs directly incurred in providing or evaluating eligible training including the costs of providing and maintaining premises and employing staff to provide support or evaluate training which is directly attributable to that training.

v) That part of the salaries of advisers and inspectors directly attributable to time spent in planning, coordinating, monitoring or evaluating eligible training.

vi) The cost of training for youth and community workers incurred by voluntary organisations may be included, provided that forms a part of the local authority's training plan submitted to the Secretary of State for approval.

Each local authority is expected to submit to the Secretary of State, a detailed proposal of an annual training plan, each year, along with a broad indication of plans for future years. The Secretary of State will determine for each local authority the maximum amount of expenditure eligible for grant aid for each national priority area and for local priorities.

The proposals submitted must relate to systematically assessed needs and priorities, set within balanced and coherent overall policies and plans and building appropriately on the strengths of current arrangements. All training supported through these arrangements must be monitored and evaluated by the authority to assess how far it has contributed to more effective and efficient delivery of the education service.

Local authorities will be expected to report in detail to the Secretary of State on the training provided and an evaluation of the effects of that training.

Local authorities are expected to demonstrate that they are collaborating closely with other interested bodies including universities, regional advisory councils and relevant voluntary organisations. They will also be expected to demonstrate, in their planning arrangements, that appropriate account is taken of the expressed needs and views of all interested parties.

The management issues

All of these forms of funding give rise to managerial and political issues, both at a local and at a national level. For example, most local education authorities are opposed to the whole principle of Education Support Grants, in which the government holds back a proportion of the Rate Support Grant and invites local education authorities to bid for money to fund projects under centrally determined headings, to which they must contribute a further 30 per cent from their own resources. Another example would be in relation to special projects for the unemployed. These are not regarded favourably by the trade unions, and in particular the Community and Youth Workers Union has persistently continued to embargo the Community Programme scheme, preventing the statutory youth service from getting as involved as it might.

For the youth service manager, therefore, the whole area of

specific projects funding is underpinned by a series of political issues, which immediately translate into managerial issues, that will impinge directly on the management and the possible outcome of any projects funded in this way.

Why use specific programme money?

The very first mangerial issue for the youth service manager, is to ask the question 'Why use specific programme money?', in order to identify both the positive and negative consequences of doing so. In my experience, that question is rarely asked. All too often, just because the money is there to be spent, bids are submitted. Furthermore, the question of who makes the decision to submit a bid is an important one.

In relation to improving the curriculum, dealing with identified educational gaps in the curriculum or coping with areas of educational disadvantage, decisions imposed by central or local government officials may well be appropriate. However, in relation to dealing with community issues or meeting community needs, it seems odd that the impetus for making a submission for specific programme funding should come from the fact that the money exists, rather than from an identification by the community of community needs.

If the first answer to the question 'Why use specific programme money?' is 'Because it's there', the second answer is usually 'Because I can't afford to pay for that project within my existing resources ...'. That second answer carries an implicit rider: '... unless I re-order my priorities and stop paying for something else and I can't or won't do that'. Yet, if the youth service manager is going to make use of specific programme funding, some prioritising and re-ordering is going to be essential, if only to identify where the local authority matching funding will come from. However, experience shows that even this exercise is often superficial, as most often the local authority contribution is solely 'in kind'. For example, the proportionate use of existing staff time already overstretched, the provided accommodation already in use for other purposes, telephone, stationery, postage, heating, lighting and cleaning costs hidden in notional allowances in special project budgets; in essence, the youth service manager may find that the project has to operate solely on the 75 per cent grant funds provided and that the local authority 25 per cent is really only notional or imaginary.

Whatever the reason for deciding to use specific programme money, it is quite clear that youth service managers are continually faced with the dilemma posed by inadequate financial resources and serious community and social problems faced by young people, which demand a response.

Much youth service resourcing is targeted on communities for purely historical reasons, which are politically difficult to change. Trying to convince the local authority elected member that the inadequate, ineffective youth club in her electoral ward should be closed down, and the resources transferred to set up a new outreach project in another ward, can be tantamount to professional suicide. Those resources have always been there, and the mistaken belief that taking them away might mean the councillor loses votes in the next election is unfortunately impossible to dispel.

So, with a continuing flow of critical needs emerging and no freedom or flexibility to review and re-order priorities in the delivery of existing resources, the youth service manager has no alternative but to make application for specific projects money. At this point another set of managerial issues emerges.

Competition or collaboration?

Within the local authority sector there has been a continuing history of territorial conflict and rigid boundary marking between local authority departments. They jealously guard their budgets, their programmes of delivery, their ownership of staff and their areas of concern and responsibility. Social and community problems are viewed through strictly departmental eyes and rarely tackled through corporate, collaborative approaches. As a consequence, when new monies are seen to be available, competition between departments to get them is intense. Too often there seems to be considerable pressure for departments to claim a problem or issue as their sole responsibility, in order to obtain specific programme funds.

In the eyes of the communities, this makes no sense at all. The 'beneficiaries' of schemes are often already alienated and highly suspicious of the local authority, and this territoriality serves only to heighten their fears and suspicions. If officers from different departments in a local authority were seen to be more actively collaborating with each other, first of all in the use of their general resources, and secondly in relation to specific programme funding, it might be possible to build some effective bridges between them and the communities they serve. Departmental collaboration might actually lead to real collaboration between departments and communities in need.

In those few examples where there are joint departmental projects, the fact that they are not rooted in a context of departmental collaboration and a corporate approach means that they are often viewed with suspicion within the collaborating departments. Often there are also real difficulties in determining lines of accountability and effective management structures for such projects.

Staff management issues

Having made the decision to establish a project funded by specific programmes money, the next serious set of issues to deal with is the recruitment, appointment and management of staff. The very nature of the issues and problems which these projects are established to respond to, and which are often a serious, urgent or critically sensitive nature, presupposes the need to recruit highly skilled, able and experienced staff. However, the fact that projects are often underfunded because of the reasons earlier stated, because they are often for a limited period of time only, and because they are aimed at the most deprived communities, with poor working conditions, it becomes increasingly difficult to recruit high calibre staff.

Furthermore, it is particularly difficult to attract high calibre black staff with appropriate qualifications and experience. Yet, if these projects are to succeed, it is essential to recruit black personnel to work in projects that are focussed on the black communities. One of the strongest criticisms of Section 11 funding is that it is targeted towards Commonwealth immigrants, and yet is most often used to employ white personnel. In the world of community politics, this has to be the equivalent of sitting on the branch that you are sawing off, and adds yet more to the alienation of deprived, disadvantaged communities from the local authorities who are supposed to represent, care for, and service them.

Where it has been possible to recruit staff to projects funded by specific programmes money, other management problems occur. The nature of short term contracts of employment, when these are used, or short term funding for projects employing staff on permanent contracts, can make the motivation and management of these staff a difficult exercise. Particularly if they are based out in the community with inadequate support services and resources, and are accountable to a youth officer based in the central civic offices or town hall.

Usually in the funding of such projects, no recognition is given to the fact that they pose an additional managerial burden for the youth service manager responsible. It will be just something else that has to be fitted into an already excessive workload. Youth officers should be asking: 'If I am going to take on the management oversight of this new project, what am I going to drop or delegate, in order to do it properly?' I would be surprised if that question ever gets asked. I would be even more surprised if it was given credence and responded to supportively by those to whom youth officers are responsible.

Monitoring, evaluation and performance indicators

Once projects are operating, and usually in the period approaching the time for re-submission, managers often begin to think about evaluation and monitoring. For a long time in the youth and community work fields, monitoring and evaluation have not been carried out systematically and have rarely been used to inform decisions about future planning and resourcing. It is vitally important, especially in relation to projects funded by specific programme money, that a more systematic approach to evaluating programmes of provision and individual practices is developed. This should take account of the basic assumptions and beliefs about the work that is being done, and the philosophical, political stance from which it is being operated.

Put at its most simple, evaluation should lead to things being done better next time. Too often, the only evaluation which seems to occur is spontaneous and intuitive by nature. It is right and proper that we should trust our intuition at times, but to rely solely on that is to do a disservice to our clients and to our employers, and it is probably the most reliable way of ensuring that neither we, nor they, nor the community get value for money.

The processes of evaluation, whatever approach is used, should be based on the assumption that the activities which are being assessed show a degree of attainment of value based objectives. In recent years, there have been considerable developments in the field of participative evaluation with which youth service managers would do well to acquaint themselves[4,5]. In a service which has an ethos of participation, it is essential to reflect that ethos in the evaluative approaches which are used.

Participative evaluation seeks to involve participants actively in the evaluation of programmes which they are participating in and to contribute to the decision-making about those and future programmes. Thus participative evaluation is a continuous process which begins in the planning stage of a project and without reserve in that all matters of direction, finance and staffing are subject to review at all times by the participants.

For many local authority managers, this will of course be anathema as it will mean that they have to give up a measure of their control. It will also mean that they will have to consult with the beneficiaries of such projects and jointly agree criteria for evaluation and suitable performance indicators. One of the major benefits that the Urban Programme funding has brought has been the insistence by central government on local consultancies and on the identification of agreed performance indicators.

Once again this poses problems for the youth service manager in allocating sufficient time, attention and commitment to this aspect of management of specific programmes. It probably also calls for special training for the majority of officers who have not developed an understanding of evaluation principles or been trained in evaluation techniques.

Termination of projects

The two basic principles of most specific programmes are: either they are designed as 'pump priming' exercises in which the beneficiaries are given a start and will gradually seek to become self-sufficient, or they are projects for which the local authority will eventually accept full responsibility.

In practice, in many cases, neither of these principles seems to survive. The dire economic and social position of many of the deprived areas and the continuing heavy demand on charitable trusts and foundations mean that specific programmes are rarely able to attract other funds in order to become self-sufficient. The withdrawal of specific programme funds usually means that projects collapse within a short period of time. The parlous state of local authority finances means that they are rarely able to consider assuming 100 per cent of the funding of such specific programmes. At some stage, therefore, the youth service manager is going to be faced with considering termination of a project or applying for continuation funds.

The effects on the communities concerned do not have to be highlighted here. What concerns me more is the effect on the youth service manager, who will probably get little support or supervision in making decisions of this nature, and whose stress levels (normally high in any case) will probably reach unacceptable heights. As with all aspects of the management of projects funded by specific programme money, the management issues and concerns for the youth service manager extend in three directions. They surround the manager in daily pursuit of the job, they extend downwards towards those being managed and upwards towards those to whom the manager is accountable, both politically and professionally. It is no wonder that many youth officers feel beleaguered in the positions they occupy.

Conclusions

I find myself unable to take a neutral, professional stance in regard to the management of specific programme funds. Although there are arguments both in favour of and in opposition to the existence of such schemes, for youth service managers the need to use them is rooted solely in the basic inadequacy of the funding of the youth service.

One of the positive arguments in favour of these schemes is that they have enabled projects to take place which otherwise would not have happened. Another is that they allow the diversion of resources to specific priority areas of need or to specialist parts of the curriculum of the youth service. It is also true that such funding has enabled people who would otherwise have remained on the dole to have work, and that it has provided opportunities for large numbers of unemployed people to involve themselves in worthwhile activities, to the benefit of their communities. Such schemes do have their value; much fine work has been done, and many individuals and communities have benefited from them.

However, the existence of specific programme funds and their use in the schemes they support clouds and hides the real issue and slows down the battle for adequate resources. Too often special projects reflect imposed solutions for communities as a response to externally assessed needs, dealt with by the process of parachuting ill-prepared troops with inadequate resources into hostile territory. They represent a series of ad hoc departmentalised approaches when what is needed are coherent, collaborative, strategic policies and co-ordinated action.

The answer surely is to carry out a radical review of the way in which youth service monies are being spent along with other departmental resources. There is clearly a need to adopt a more effective targeting approach for those sectors of the adolescent community who most need the attention of the youth service. I would suggest that making better use of mainstream resources is more appropriate than making ineffective use of specific programmes money.

Youth service managers should only attempt to use specific programme money if they can do so collaboratively with the communities to benefit and the other local authority departments, in such a way that it complements the use of their mainstream resources. That will demand giving proper management attention to the specific programmes area of work and allocating an appropriate amount of time and resources to managing it. If the youth service manager cannot give programmes the management time they deserve, they should be avoided.

The Thompson Report[6] highlighted a continuing criticism of the management of the youth service. When one looks at the size of the job that needs to be done, the actual status and position of youth officers in the decision-making hierarchy, the low level of general resources and the lack of management training available, it is no wonder that there continue to be managerial problems.

One of the more important training lessons to be learned by any manager is to develop the ability to be able to say 'no' and not to continue taking on more and more just because it is there to be done. If we look at the history of a number of organisations which have failed, one ot the common factors leading to their failure is that of being seduced by money. Funds suddenly become available, the organisation grabs the funds and engages in new work without reorganising its management substructure or reducing its original workload. The organisation then discovers that it has diverted from its original goals and principles and is doing something which it was not set up or equipped to do, and collapses. An important lesson for all organisations to learn is not to be seduced by money.

However, I suspect that because the funding of the youth service is so woefully inadequate, it is probable that most youth officers are not going to be able to resist being seduced by hot money. I would suggest that they need to remember that hot money will burn holes in their pockets and needs to be handled with extreme care[7].

References

1. Jones, M (1986), *Government Grants: an NCVO Practical Guide*, Bedford Square Press.
2. Oldfield, C (1987), *Community Service Responses to Unemployment*, National Youth Bureau.
3. (1986) *Local Education Authority Training Grants Scheme – Financial Year 1987-8*, DES Circular 6/86, Department of Education and Science.
4. Ruddock, R (1981), *Evaluation: a Consideration of Principles and Methods*, Manchester Monographs Ltd, University of Manchester.
5. (1986), *NYB Resources and Reading List on Evaluation*, National Youth Bureau.
6. The Thompson Report (1982), *Experience and Participation, The Report of the Review Group on the Youth Service*, Command 8686, HMSO.
7. Hope, P (1987), *Ideas into Action: a Practical Guide to Managers Setting up Special Projects*, National Council for Voluntary Youth Services.

10 Management of a national agency

Tanner Shields

Brave enough to get on board;
Quick enough to stay ahead of the field;
Skilful enough to stay in the race avoiding what could be a fatal mistake in bumping into others,
Yet sensitive enough to know when to brake so as to stay on the right track;

But, as in most situations, the race is won not by power alone but by the skill of doing the right thing at the right time. This needs a powerful back-up team which ensures that the 'machine' works to maximum efficiency.

Successful national management means that the whole team, whether directly in the line-management of the national body or whether independently employed at a different level must be motivated, serviced and, above all, supported.

I work for a national voluntary youth organisation of some 50,000 members which had its roots in training future farmers. Because this training included a more expanded curriculum such as public speaking and craft training, it contained an interesting and broad programme content and thus attracted a wide range of interests. The most significant factor however was that from early days in the 1920's those of membership age were the only people with power to vote at club level to choose their programmes and to elect people forward to represent them.

The modern Young Farmers' Club (YFC) therefore has its member democracy as its very foundation. This forms the background to YFC actions and thus to my thinking in writing this chapter. As the chief national staff member, my power is limited to that given to maintain the legal and charitable status. On policy and activities I have to work to influence any changes 'National' would like to see made. I have tried to bring these principles to the National Council for Voluntary Youth Services during my six years as vice chairman.

To write on the management of a national agency is to invite criticism. There are great difficulties in reflecting different types of organization, but these are nothing compared with those of delivering a national programme locally.

Working for a national agency it is easy to think of the national body as something apart, the demands of which must be met by those at ground level. The reverse must be our criteria. The national agency is there to serve the ground level youth work providers. So the management, as well as responding to good techniques in a business sense, also has to be ultra-sensitive to the effect of any particular style on those people on whom we depend to deliver the ultimate programme.

We manage with one eye in each direction: one to ensure that we are efficient in the whole range of management skills, such as the maintenance of a streamlined structure, adequate financial control and maximising the use of available assets; the other ensuring that through excellent communication, staff development policies, leadership and training, we are able to inspire those who serve the same organisation at a different level.

The object of management

Our management must ensure we achieve the movement's objectives as effectively as possible within the resources available to us. In administrative aspects we should seek to be efficient. However, the real function of a youth organisation is the personal development of its members and a really important part of this can be achieved by the involvement of the members in the decision-making processes – if possible all the way through to the national structure. In these circumstances management must firstly be effective in seeking and managing resources and secondly must ensure that the decision-making within the management structure involves as many people as possible in a meaningful process of learning.

Therefore, though I hope that it is effective on behalf of the membership it serves, my management is not as good as I could, in theory, make it, simply because the task is to involve as many people as possible to as high a level as possible in the decision-making process.

Most organisations respond to different management styles; indeed, many of them are in need of a particular style. My organisation is one of the few where the demands on the national body are made directly by members. This process can go as far as the members having the freedom to change the whole ethos of the organisation. This creates an insatiable need for information. Its value is that it gives us the opportunity to reflect more accurately the requirements of today's young people.

Most national youth work agencies have specific values which have been part of their ethos since foundation days. While maintaining these values, we have to respond to changing attitudes and to the circumstances which prevail as we approach the 21st century.

There are specific expectations of our agencies. Some arise simply because the agency exists, some are created by the standing and influence of that body, while others are created by what it sets out to achieve. All this adds up to constantly increasing pressure and the need to set clear priorities. In making such judgements one fact must be kept in mind: that the end product of the work, be it at national, regional, county or local level, must be the delivery of better youth work for the individual young person. We must also remember that no-one is 'national'; we are all local to somewhere – even if some of us assume wider national responsibilities, these usually result in action by local people.

Different national agencies

As there are many different types of national agency, it is difficult to write about one particular type or any particular method of delivery. The principles of good management are well known, but these have to be relevant to the circumstances created by the structures of the organisation and, particularly, the lines of authority.

In some organisations the power for virtually all decisions is vested in the chief executive, who has a very broad remit within which to work, much like the managing director of a firm. At the other end of the scale, there are organisations where the staff simply carry out functions for various committees, some of which are elected, others fairly autocratic and self-perpetuating. Between the extremes there are many other models: in some the policies are decided by national committees and reflected downwards – in some this process is reversed. Others are federations of autonomous groups which again need a different style of management.

Many new organisations in the youth service are so small that their operation is no more than one person with very little administrative support. Some of these have traditional values while some must be recognised as a new type of youth service, often evolving in the inner cities and working with disadvantaged groups. While we find it hard to look upon them as national bodies at the moment, we must realise that some will grow to cover wide areas of work and of the country. Delivery of their service will be even more difficult as they expand, with or without structures, to carry their youth work into more challenging situations. While considering 'national bodies', we must be conscious of the environment of tomorrow, the demands of which may be met by different methods. Our minds must be open to recognise the new challenges and to support those colleagues in the youth service who meet new needs in different ways.

Working at national level

The strongest national programmes are devised by local people coming together nationally, spread throughout the network, and implemented locally.

It is important for someone working at 'national' to have an understanding of the pressures on those who deliver the face-to-face youth work. However, this is also true the other way round and it is more often the case that those who work at local levels do not have an understanding of the role or the pressures of working from a national agency.

The politics of being national cause real emotional difficulties which have to be overcome. It is a fact of life that most people think of national as something remote and distinctly irrelevant to their work. They do not believe that people who work at national have the same kind of personal commitment to the coal face work, so the word creates an inbuilt prejudice which has to be overcome before a real partnership can develop. Overcoming these politics is a time-consuming task which takes a great deal of personal commitment but it is an essential piece of groundwork, before delivery of programmes can really be effective. We must be sensitive to this feeling in all our work and seek to lower the barriers.

Aims must be established and publicised, so that all involved know what the national organisation is attempting to achieve. These are likely to be contained in a national policy statement which, in order to obtain total commitment to its principles, will be developed by discussion throughout the whole organisation before approval at an annual general meeting. While being flexible enough to meet changing circumstances, a policy statement will set the parameters within which the national agency develops its more short term objectives.

These objectives, being more specific, are achieved through the programmes which are the stepping stones we use to achieve our objectives. However, setting objectives, then developing practical programmes to achieve these, will fail unless adequate training is incorporated into the system for both the structure to be managed effectively and the programmes to be achieved to a satisfying level of competence.

Involving the members

I have long since learned of the fallacy that members are excluded from participation in national youth organisations. A closer look will reveal that the opportunities for young people in the decision-making and thus the management of their national organisations is far greater than we think. However, the actual progress that young people have made in achieving more say is less praiseworthy. The blame for this is often laid at the doors of the structures or of the old traditionalists who have 'seized power'. This is also far from the truth in most cases.

Our failures in member involvement are fourfold: firstly, we fail to convince most young people that involvement in management and decision-making is important to them; secondly, we fail to carry out sufficient training to ensure that members are equipped to take an equal part in the decision-making process; thirdly, we fail to give the political education to enable members to hold their own in the structures through which they must work. Fourthly, too many of our meetings fit the professional timetable, not the volunteers'.

Involving young people in management is to set them up for some level of failure, unless the opportunity is offered in a realistic way. This not only involves training but also a great deal of thought on timetabling and financial support so that they can be involved on an equal footing with the adults involved. Regrettably, because of our failure to do the groundwork, our offers to young people to get involved in the process rarely leave us overwhelmed with offers.

Establishing and maintaining communications

A national organisation must avoid the trap of believing that communication and publicity should merely be directed outside to tell the world at large about our organisation. With an ever-changing young membership and a very large number of volunteers to keep informed, internal publicity is even more important.

Attempting to inform a membership through the formal lines of communication in a representative body is doomed to failure, but success can be achieved by stories printed in national and local press which give a flavour of the organisation and talk about specific issues. This publicity material will bring the full context of our organisation to our members as much as it will to the general public.

The written word

Inevitably we send reports and minutes throughout our structures and these have some effect in briefing people. However, for full information there is a vast quantity to be read, and unfortunately people are inundated with uninspiring material which they often do not read.

Abridged reports of sub-committee minutes and council minutes give us the opportunity to prepare what is in effect a brief for delegates on the most pertinent points which have to be relayed. These can be copied at other levels for onward transmission. However, such documents inevitably do not put the flavour of the arguments, and communications on vital issues need to be augmented by more specific material than this.

We are not alone in the race to outdo each other in producing gimmicky colourful attractive leaflets to be found among the deluge which lands on our doormats daily. Few people read much in detail but colour and design can help greatly.

Personal contact

Creating the interest in people to want to know about the work of the organisation is an essential ingredient before effective reading is likely to take place. This can be helped by personal contact and, depending on the size of the organisation and its structures, discussion and conference-type activity is an important part of a national staff member's role in communication. It not only enables the facts to be discussed but also gives a chance to enthuse and break down barriers which inhibit effective communication.

Communicating with a large number of people needs specific skills and rarely reaches maximum effect. Thus, the regional structure within a national body gives scope for communicating with smaller groups and for our staff or volunteers at that level, when thoroughly briefed, to act as an effective personal link in the lines of communication.

Using the media

Much, but not all of, the media seeks only sensational news. The 'six in a bed' type story will always find an outlet but serious newspapers and specialist magazines are also looking for the right material to interest their readers, who may well be parents of our prospective members. Writing good unused material is time-consuming and frustrating. However, if unused it is rarely wasted. How much effort do we put into this aspect of work? How often have we asked for a specific page in a relevant specialist magazine? Do we all suggest providing local radio programmes – perhaps attached to incoming international visitors' receptions, so that we can publicise our programmes? How often do we push our 'groups' onto TV game shows?

The up-to-date personalised press release is a start but only succeeds if followed up on the right occasions by personal contact and a stream of practical ideas for action.

Organisation & planning of work

It is essential to develop individual work plans for staff. Generalised job descriptions and specifications are not enough. While the individual people are kind, it is all too easy for the system to become a cruel taskmaster and create demands without thought to the workload on staff. Having first written the 'policy statement' type of document, we have next produced a five-year plan or, as it could be called, a manifesto. However, this will be written in general terms and is not nearly specific enough for work planning on a shorter term basis.

Even 12-month work plans can be too general for the realities of actually doing a job. They are time-consuming to produce and can ask the individual operating the plan to ignore that which is pressing, most urgent and new, in favour of what seemed most relevant yesterday. Plans cannot substitute for daily management of personal time and a person who is on top of their job must be given the freedom to do that job in the light of current circumstances. Their most critical challenge will be to say 'no' to something which comes through the door on the day. There has to be planning and control within a management structure but it is important that work plans do not inhibit people from tackling the right job at the right time, but rather that they guide them to work within the remit given to best effect. My ideal planning structure for an organisation is:

A national policy statement agreed by the organisation followed by commitment from regional and county levels to the principles of that policy statement.

This should be followed by the development of practical programmes at national, regional, county and local levels which guide the movement to fulfil the whole spectrum contained within the policy statement.

The policy, together with the practical programmes, then needs a training strategy throughout the organisation to enable everyone involved to understand their role and achieve maximum success. There is little value in having a well-planned, balanced programme if this is not put into practice efficiently. This needs an administration which is simple and as thorough as possible. It must not be officious or over-formal but, conversely, the attempts to create a good atmosphere must not lead to sloppy systems.

Timing

The lead time for a national organisation wanting its programmes operated through a local group will mean that region, county and club must have the information to build into their forward plans at an appropriate time. A sensitive national agency knows the kind of planning going on at local level and knows the necessary timetable so that national plans can be incorporated locally. If you miss these deadlines, 'national' becomes a burden to local workers and the impetus for action through to national level is likely to be lost.

Delegation

Successful management depends on motivating other people, yet as with so many things there is the danger that the same few do everything. Either we have convinced too few people that what we are doing is right or we have not involved committee members and staff in such a way that they feel able to assume responsibility for what is decided. Obtaining people's commitment is vital and involves them in understanding the same concepts and working towards the same goals as the national body. Responsibility can be delegated and should be given in a meaningful way right down the line. Whatever our structure the responsibility to lead and inspire is shared with other levels. The responsibility for nationally planned programmes, if taken on at other levels, must be delegated, and the national body cannot and should not seek to interfere with their operation. Delegation must be carried out in a way which ensures that the person to whom we delegate understands the whole task and is responsible for its successful completion. In that way lies personal satisfaction and commitment.

Setting standards

We often see our personal example reflected in those around us.
Many sectors of an organisation look at the national body to provide
the lead and it is important that this lead is seen to be right. Though
there are constant changes in values and different methods become
more in vogue, some things are constant.

Courtesy is of paramount importance and must be shown to
everyone on all occasions, whatever the provocation. The ten
commandments of a good leader finish by saying 'though shalt not
murder, though you may feel like it most of the time'. This may be
slightly over-the-top, but it contains a great deal of feeling. A person's
impression, particularly of a national organisation, might be judged
by one single encounter and simple friendship and courtesy in
dealings with all result not only in a more civilised conduct of our
affairs, but also in real money in the bank in the long term. We should
expect the same courtesy in return.

The quality of our personal input adds to the essential quality of
what we provide. Though it is inevitable that measurement of our
quality will be subjective, our clients judge.

Role of a professional working with committees and with volunteers

Most of us delivering a local programme through a national agency
are working through committees. The skill of making committees
work is the subject for a great deal of training material and
effectiveness is greatly enhanced when we avail ourselves of this and
master the skills of putting it into practice. Committees are an
essential part of the decision-making process. They relay to the
manager the requirements of the whole organisation as far as
philosophy and practical programmes are concerned, and they are
communication channels the other way. Committees are not always,
in fact not often, the best way to make effective decisions but they do
give us the best opportunity yet devised of developing ideas, relaying
information and giving a forum for debate.

Our decision-making systems may well be helped with the advent
of electronic communications directly into the homes of our
members. Even when they are, our committee structure will survive
to develop the ideas and people's commitment to the national
agency. Without such commitment there is no chance of successful
delivery so we owe it to ourselves and our committee members to be
more effective in planning, organisation, support and administration
so that the decision-making processes and the whole effect of what

we are trying to do is enhanced. I attend many meetings where the pre-planning and the real communication is so bad that the majority of decisions are made by default, for example, 23 votes in favour, four against with 35 abstentions.

An informed committee membership is vital as a committee's decisions will reflect the information it is given. A committee which knows less than its chair and secretary is a burden on the system, not a help.

It is therefore incumbent upon us to do all we can to involve our committee members, to create a good atmosphere, to give every scrap of information we can, and to ensure there are no secrets – that traditional block which stops people ever really getting to grips with what we do. In this way, people can play a full part in the decision-making process. We must also free sufficient time to spend with members of our committees and with other people working at ground level. They must feel our personal support.

The decision-making process through a national organisation must be co-ordinated. County meetings must see the agendas of regional meetings and regional meetings must see the agendas for national meetings. It is vital that each level of the organisation is given the opportunity to discuss the agenda of the next level, thus influencing decisions rather than receiving a report. Proactive not reactive. Through this two-way process, delegates coming forward to national bodies will reflect ground level opinion and commit ground level support to policies. If we merely send reports of decisions and expect the whole body of opinion to follow in our footsteps, we are setting ourselves up for certain failure.

I liken the process of communication through a committee structure as pouring material into a funnel. In our organisation we hold four-day meetings in Europe which are poured back into a national council meeting as a 10 minute report. The council report given back to the county executive committee may be 10 minutes long and may well not contain any aspect of the report from Europe. The report from the county executive committee to the local club will last from three to five minutes and has virtually no chance of containing any aspect of the European meeting. We must be conscious of the shortcomings of such a system, and consider how we are going to augment the passing of information so that new and minority interests are not blocked out. At the moment it is nothing short of a miracle, if such minority interest material available in national programmes is communicated to the local group.

Too often members are given the conclusions of sub-committees and asked to approve the decisions. There is no way that this can be realistically done unless they have read the reasoning behind the decision. Some committees may wish to nod through the recommendations while others will find it impossible to give support at ground level unless they have at least had the opportunity to familiarise themselves with the arguments.

It is as important to create the right committee environment as it is to create a good 'club' atmosphere. How often do we hear that the best decisions are made in the coffee bar after the meeting? Has the chair failed to conduct the meeting properly or should the meeting have generated the coffee bar atmosphere? Attention to correct meeting procedures must not dampen a free and relaxed debating atmosphere.

Staff roles & management

As in all organisations, selection of the right staff is critical, particularly acknowledging the very different circumstances in which the staff of some voluntary organisations work. Even though they work for charities and for voluntary organisations, these two words should not be used to indicate that anything less than maximum efficiency is acceptable. Good management of staff and professional appraisal of their performance is essential to a voluntary organisation. Such appraisal systems have been developed for use within the youth service. Staff development policies, including the structures by which expectations will be identified, are available in most organisations, and advice is available from the Council for Education and Training in Youth and Community Work (CETYCW). Such advice is invaluable, particularly to small organisations who can obtain top level help at little or no cost and so establish correct employment structures. My only concern is that in management of our own time and that of the team, we do not completely bog ourselves and our committees down in such a morrass of planning and re-planning that we lose sight of the original objectives.

The appointment procedures and basic documentation, such as job descriptions, job specifications and terms of employment, must be correctly set down. They will not only guide the staff as to what the employers expect, but they will be the criteria on which performance appraisal will be based. Our organisation sets down a timetable for performance appraisal which involves regular appraisals in the first few months of the job, with the frequency decreasing to an annual appraisal, or more regularly if requested by either party.

Staff management in a committee structure can be complicated. There are various patterns of line management. In my organisation, these come through the voluntary members, some of whom are lacking in staff management experience. Some of the committees are far too large to fulfil current requirements of employment legislation. With the advent of this legislation, management committees have taken a firm hold in most voluntary organisations, and I believe these are essential for the proper employment of professional staff, particularly within a member democracy. The only danger is that we insulate our staff from the feelings of the people for whom they work.

Many staff in the youth service have to be self-motivating and to work on their own initiative. Part of an appraisal system is to obtain a deep knowledge of the work in which our staff are involved. It is all too easy for staff to lose sight of the original objectives of their work and to be drawn into very worthy side issues. When the organisation has set its objectives and given the staff a brief, there has to be an appraisal of the output to ensure that the whole organisation can take maximum benefit from the product. It is possible to produce too much, or to produce our work in the wrong way, so that it is not being utilised. Similarly, most agencies would be pleased if they could afford an increase in staff time to carry out their work – the pressure is always there. However, we must ensure that whatever work we create at national level can be turned into programme content by the different levels of the organisation or, however worthy, we become irrelevant.

The chief officer

The role of the chief officer, as team leader, is critical for any agency. The successful chief officer must lead the organisation, its policy, aims and objectives. He or she must ensure the highest level of management skills so that the organisation is run efficiently and time and money is spent effectively in achieving the agreed policy. The pitfalls are numerous, but one great danger is of being drawn into the wrong priorities and becoming so over-committed that good judgement goes and one fails to work on the things which could be most effective.

Michael Butterfield, recently chief executive of the National Association of Youth Clubs, speaking to the chief officers of the national voluntary organisations at the HMI Conference in 1986, analysed the work of chief officers under three major heading:

1. Working inside the organisation
(a) As leader, manager and supporter of the staff team on policy development, innovation and planning;
   We have to note that in a changing society, with changing attitudes, it is essential that the organisation changes to keep up-to-date;

(b) providing an information service to president and honorary officers, sub-committee chairs, etc;
(c) service to council, executive committee and various sub-committees;
(d) information and an advisory service to regions, counties and occasionally local groups;
(e) financial control and budgeting;
(f) fund-raising;
(g) writing and publishing various material.

2. Externally
(a) relationships with government departments and HMI;
(b) working with the wider youth service for relationships and information, debating policy and keeping the organisation an integral part of the youth provision; This involves a great deal of reading so as to provide an information service to your organisation;
(c) links with those outside the youth service which have a particular relationship with your organisation;
(d) fund-raising and meeting the publicity and support needs of sponsors.

3. Balance

It is extremely difficult to keep the right balance between internal and external work. Needs change, and it is very difficult to change emphasis quickly enough.

All these things, together with the need to learn enough to do the job and to keep up-to-date, add up to the need for a large input of knowledge, skill and time. We must inevitably fail in some places some of the time, and the need to keep back the day-to-day administration in order to have time to think is crucial.

Finances

Some chief officers have a major part to play in the management of the finances of their organisation. Others are well protected from this and need do no other than ensure that they work within the budgets. The larger the organisation the more likely it is that financial planning will be available through other officers. To ensure financial stability every agency must ensure that its finance is raised, is allocated according to policy and that adequate budgetary control is exercised by all individuals and committees. Different organisations have their own methods of raising money and their own favourite sources to which they apply. None are easily achieved.

Fund-raising from grants, private trusts and from public funds is well documented through publications such as the *Directory of Grant Making Trusts*[1]. Fund-raising from industry is more problematical but is possible, for those prepared to find the right contacts, to understand the company objectives and to set out their case accordingly.

From whatever source revenue comes, it has to be worked for, justified and well husbanded. Members, no less than sponsors or grant sources, demand that their money is accounted for and used according to their wishes. Some sponsors or donors, once having agreed the objective of the expenditure, will be very easy about detailed management of a project and, though supportive, will not expect to be closely involved. Others look in more detail at the effect of their support and require a higher profile and a greater involvement. Finding sponsors for national events is sometimes easier than looking after the sponsorship and ensuring that the expectations of all those involved are thoroughly met. One political problem is that sponsors' requirements have to be balanced against the desire of the organisation to be politically and commercially unbiased. It is not unknown for the needs of a national sponsor to be opposed at local level.

Fund-raising from public funds is ever more difficult, particularly as criteria are inclined to change. At the moment the change is away from core funding and towards work which tackles the difficult issues facing modern society – unemployment and discrimination, for example.

If the youth service is to carry out work on behalf of young people, then it has to be adequately funded. Many of those in 'power' are not playing the game with the youth service and maybe that is our fault, through lack of political pressure and not creating a high enough profile. We see the government's response to the Thompson Report boasting about the effectiveness of the work of the voluntary sector with six million young people involved, yet there isn't a single sentence in the government Circular 1.85 which puts more resources into general youth work, either to enable that work to be expanded, or to tackle the new work which a changing society inevitably brings. Even worse, the suggestion is that to tackle the new challenges we should divert resources from existing expenditure. This must inevitably mean some dimunuition of the mainstream youth work, rocking the very base from which we work. Surely this mut be a wrong policy. It is only from a strong base that we can make an effective contribution to meet the changing demands of today's society.

It is my opinion that our work of building an image for the youth service to improve our credibility with educationalists and in parliament has, by and large, failed. We have little clout and we need to be a great deal more effective to survive. While we have little muscle, we have a great deal of quality in our work and natural justice on our side. We also have emotive support from a wide sector of the community. We must play these cards for all they are worth and embarrass members of the government so that, if they fail to support us, they are seen publicly to be undermining the values for which the youth service has fought, in many instances single-handed, to uphold. Those of us who lead national youth service agencies today need to fight for resources as hard as our founders fought to establish the organisations. If we believe enough in our role in the 21st century, we will be prepared to take this on board now, while we still have our base.

Links with others and umbrella bodies

Managers of national agencies are drawn into links with government and national agencies and with a number of umbrella bodies. The value of these umbrella bodies can be considerable, particularly to small organisations. Nonetheless, one has to be extremely careful that involvement in such bodies and in other activities which are on the fringe of the mainstream of our work, does not subsume the staff of the organisation and result in a failure to manage our own time and achieve the objectives of our own work. Umbrella bodies can perform important partnership functions for us:

(a) they enable us to meet, work with and discuss problems with people who are in similar circumstances and who have to respond to similar pressures;

(b) they provide a service to organisations, condensing the vast amount of information from the Youth Service sector, putting it into short, readable form and giving the reference where more detailed material is available;

(c) they enable us to meet together to broaden our own thinking and knowledge of a wider society;

(d) they enable us to join together to speak far more strongly to Government and conversely, they enable Government to have one avenue through which it can speak to the voluntary sector;

(e) they enable us on a personal basis to meet friends and colleagues in similar work which is emotionally supportive and gives us a stronger personal platform from which to work in our own organisation.

Umbrella bodies have a vital role to play, but it is incumbent upon us to make sure that our organisation is adequately represented on such bodies to make use of the opportunity. We must give sufficient importance to the day-to-day work of these umbrella bodies to ensure that they are not becoming an end unto themselves rather than an asset to the voluntary sector.

The value can be immense. If we do not make use of this or if our reasons for being members are not met, we usually have only ourselves to blame for not fully taking part in the process.

Training

I cannot write a chapter on delivery of programmes without underlining the paramount importance of the training being geared to enable the national body to achieve its goals.

Whatever the ethos of the organisation, its aims, objectives or its practical programmes, it is only as good as the performance of all those who have a function within it. Too often, because of the nature of our organisation, we feel that we should not ask too much of the volunteers within the system. I believe that we should ask for much more training. We put too many people into positions where for one reason or another they are not able to be successful. The thing I believe could help most towards greater youth work success is training. The majority of people expect to be trained to perform well at work. Why then do we expect so many who walk into different levels of responsibility in our organisations to react intuitively and be successful. I would love to be complimentary about youth service training. Most of the conference-type gatherings achieve something and similarly staff training sessions have a certain effect on improving performance. However, too much of present training is missing the mark. My experience is that while staff feel it is their duty to attend some training and do gain from it, particularly through open discussion of their work, most members cannot be dragged there except under threat. I have worked professionally and voluntarily for 20 years in three organisations and the standard response to getting members to attend outside training sessions in youth work has been negative. The unwary may be persuaded to go once but any attempt to get them forward for a second 'dose of medicine' will be met by a mass stampede in the opposite direction.

'Training must be done and it can be fun' is the slogan coined by David Richardson, YFC's National Training Officer. He makes it fun. We must enable people to achieve a high standard and this will only be achieved with good training which leads to good practice and good experiences in our youth groups.

Training is the least popular of our youth service activities, but far and away the most important. If good training can be achieved, the members are more than competent to provide good practical activities through which most of the personal development will take place. We will hold members longer if their minds are exercised by planning their own youth service, in addition to organising the practical activities in which they ask to participate.

My national organisation is 20 years late in developing a national training strategy which will ensure that the members, volunteers and staff all independently employed at the different levels, are drawn together in an effective training team, planning together the objectives we set and ensuring that everyone along the line is helped to fulfil their part to the maximum of their ability.

The training strategy is the way of using all our resources as efficiently as possible to the identified target of improving the standard of youth work at ground level. The personal development will come as a result of the experiences members have and these experiences can be improved by better ground level work. It will make our service more attractive and a better understood partner in the education service, the role in which we could gain more credence in future years. 'Tool box' and skills training to run our local groups, 'concepts' training to broaden the traditional programmes so that we give more people a satisfactory experience, and training so that our planning and management gives us a better chance of implementing these things properly, are the training agenda which we should lay before every national organisation.

My organisation offers training which ranges from personal skills in sport, crafts, displays and speaking, through to political education and language training at European level. We cannot expect miracles on behalf of all our members, but the youth service has this range of educational value for young adults and I fear that we are failing to sell our product to the vast majority of those who may be interested, with the result that we are too often written off. A well-implemented training strategy would give better performance and give us more credence in all fields.

We listen closely to what others in our agency are saying and though we do our best to influence their thinking and to provide leadership, at the end of the debate we can only be effective if we respond to ground level needs. That principle is true no matter whether we talk about a national agency influencing ground level programmes or whether we talk about a county statutory youth service responding to local clubs.

A few years' experience has taught those of us working for national agencies to practise a great deal of humility. We soon discover that simple is most effective and very little of what the

Messiah preaches is practised, at least in the short term. However, you must forgive us if we preach a little – we need to lead the national agencies into the 21st century.

Reference

1. *Directory of Grant Making Trusts*, Charities Aid Foundation.

11 Support and training of managers

Michael Cox

'Courses for current and prospective youth officers; a beginning has been made in certain regions with courses for newly appointed officers, but this needs to be much more widely spread. There is also a need for refresher courses and specialist courses for officers already in post'[1].

'... newly appointed officers, often promoted from youth work or teaching posts, are placed in generalist roles which require of them a comprehensive range of managerial, communication, organisational and advisory skills ... it is of concern that there is no preparatory or in-service training nor any regular professional supervision of an individual officer's work to encourage a more effective interpretation of the role'[2].

'The step from field worker to youth and community education officer needs to be bridged. It would not be inappropriate to view the transition as a career change. Whilst clearly it is not a career change in the sense that the individual is still working within the same service, the nature of the work, the environment, the structure and the expectations of others will be different.'[3]

'The need remains to ensure that the (youth) service is managed to best effect. Earlier reports have drawn attention to this need but for whatever reason initiatives have been confined to a few local developments. The Commission stresses the paramount importance of preparatory and in-service training for youth officers to be introduced on the basis of local delivery to a national standard' Cmnd. 9396 'Youth Services for the 21st Century' 1996.

A flight of fantasy?

A stark reality?
A printers' error?

No, not a printers' error; certainly an exercise in fantasy but a fantasy which has roots in reality.

The readers of this book will have discovered that reality. A reality which ensures that the youth worker is relatively well served through staff development programmes, through in-service education and training and through experiential learning opportunities. These support and training systems are essentially designed to assist the individual worker in improving performance and delivery as a youth worker. The staff development programmes are largely geared towards this end and seek to reconcile the task as perceived by the worker, the task as perceived by the manager, resourcing constraints and job satisfaction.

Career development is acknowledged. But acknowledgement alone is not enough – career guidance has its place, but once agreement is reached about realistic career hopes, what help is given, in practical terms, to prepare the worker who wishes to move into the officer role for the significant changes that such a role brings?

The reader who has journeyed through the preceding pages will, by now, have defined a set of training needs and will have some view as to how those needs should be met. The fact that such needs remain largely unmet lies in the hands of that cadre of people known as youth officers in post. Often for the most laudable of reasons resources are placed everywhere but towards youth officer training. This is not due to an unhealthy and Victorian collusion between officers and employers, but rather to a combination of a desire to ensure that maximum resources are directed towards young people and those who work directly with them, and to a feeling promoted in so many hierarchical structures that the more senior the post the more self-contained the post holder.

It is a brave manager indeed who says to an employing agency that non-managerial supervision is an essential tool in enabling him or her to manage effectively. Yet the importance of this is recognised for other staff, so why not for the youth officer?

This chapter cannot survey the current arrangements for the support and training of managers for they do not, to any consistent extent, exist. You, the reader, will have defined such needs and the responsibility is now yours – a responsibility to be brave enough to shout for getting your own needs met and for ensuring that those who follow your career path are better prepared than you were.

Areas of education and training

In order to define the areas of education and training that a newly
appointed officer requires, it is necessary to be clear about the
purpose of such education. Is it:

- – to prepare individuals for their first management roles, so that
  managers can perform their jobs more efficiently and effectively?
- – to prepare for increased responsibility?
- – to gain extra transferable skills?
- – to achieve greater personal happiness and satisfaction?

The training content should include information and skill-
enhancement for present jobs, preparation for job-change and future
responsibilities and the development of behaviour which will meet
the personal needs of managers. It is suggested that an
understanding of the principles of management, skill in the
application of management techniques, regular updating, forecasting
and planning opportunities need to be built into any serious training
programme for youth service management.

Management training should include a sound understanding of
what management is and what it is not. Too often it is confused with
administration and bureaucracy. It should be a systematic approach
to realising the full potential of all resources – especially people – to
work towards clearly defined goals. The basic functions of
management – planning, organising, directing, co-ordinating and
controlling – are well documented and have been applied to every
kind of organisation. A wealth of literature and training materials
exists ready for use in the training of youth service managers.

We all probably have cherished notions about management style
and techniques which are founded on prejudice rather than on reality
or which a good deal of research has proved to be fallacious. In the
absence of training most managers learn their management
behaviour by copying other managers, and whilst this has some
merit it is clearly random and dependent upon the quality or
appropriateness of the 'model'. Some of the management techniques
of senior officers may be more appropriate to an expanding
educational provision than to the contracting one in which people
now work – yet the styles and techniques have not always changed
and new officers are still expected to learn from older colleagues with
little alternative training on offer.

There is a serious danger in restricting the content of in-service
training to management techniques, with the implication that youth
and community officers have a role simply in managing service
delivery. It is important to recognise their role of professional
leadership too. Assuming that people of sound professional ability

are appointed to officer posts, they have an obligation to influence the determination of objectives, to inform practice and to advise on its delivery.

There is a richness in the variety of educational provision in this country. The youth service benefits from the diversity of approaches in every local authority and the many voluntary organisations. But there is no merit in constantly re-inventing the wheel, and it is wasteful not to share experience and work together for improvement. Senior managers of Britain's youth service must be more than the servants of policies. They must be able to influence policies so that the service can be effective in its tasks. They are, after all, best placed and do have an obligation to advise employing agencies and local authorities about youth work policy.

Learning on the job has many advantages but has its limitations too. Not every job encompasses the whole range of youth work variety and many managers will have had little or no direct experience of some changes or developments. Those who have been working for a long time in rural counties may not have had to deal with Section 11 or Urban Programme funding, for instance, and those in large cities may know little about the particular disadvantages of rural young people. On more than one occasion senior officers have commented that candidates for more senior posts often had little direct experience of some of the issues confronting a service to which they were applying. The absence of any comprehensive and systematic programme of training for managers in the service exacerbates this problem.

Looking at the tasks which officers in the youth and community service are required to carry out will highlight some of the skills necessary for those tasks. In turn this will suggest some areas of training which must figure in a programme for officers. A recent survey of the work done by area officers – often the first management post – suggest that these tasks are mainly concerned with diagnostic formulation, evaluative and communication skills.

The content of appropriate training for managers should include an examination of the state of young people's world and some exploration of the implications for young people of the changes which have occurred in society over the past twenty years. These changes would include high unemployment, longer education and training, the move from manufacturing to service industry, technological advance in communications, a growth in the proportion of international companies and organisations. On the social scene there are higher expectations of women and ethnic minority groups – many of whom are second or third generation British – increasing urban decay, deterioration in rural community services, increasing numbers of one-parent families and stepfamilies, the advent of new and more worrying sexually-transmitted diseases, an alienation of many young people towards the police force, changes in the law which affect young people, an apparent polarisation in political and moral values and an arrest in the reduction of class differences. Such profound changes affecting young people clearly ensure that they have to be considered in the training of youth service managers.

Whether in local education authorities or in voluntary organisations the youth service officer/manager is at the interface between the field and the resource-providers. A basic principle of community education is the encouragement of community groups – including young people – to determine their own needs and to be challenging establishment groups to make better provision or to change their practices to enable legitimate access to policy-making. Since any change entails a departure from the status quo this will often be seen as a threat to or criticism of those who hold power at present, and so the officer will frequently find him/herself in a difficult professional situation. Because of this it is important that the regular training programme includes support mechanisms to handle the stress that may result.

Effective performance of managers will depend, too, upon them being reasonably happy people who gain an adequate level of job satisfaction. Attention to personal physical and psychological well-being is not an expensive and luxurious perk but makes sound economic sense in any enterprise and most particularly in one which is as dependent as the youth service upon the goodwill of its workforce. So the training must take account of personal needs for job happiness, absence of anxieties about the future such as retirement preparation, opportunity for personal updating on professional issues by reading and thinking time, support mechanisms and self-management strategies for coping with stress, boredom and exhaustion.

To summarise, the content of training should include management principles and techniques, the place of professional leadership, the development of diagnostic, evaluative and communication skills, a broad examination of the service in different settings, changes in the world of young people, policy formulation by senior officers, preparation for roles of greater responsibility and personal support mechanisms.

What form of training?

A mistake commonly made is to equate training with training courses. A course is a discrete programme of training, usually but not always undertaken away from the normal working environment, although it will often have elements which relate to the normal work of the student. A comprehensive programme of training will include courses and the opportunity to pursue them. Reference has already been made here to the need for training which can best be done on courses. But that is only a part of the programme and there are other ways of offering training. In their report on the Welsh youth service the Welsh HMIs said '... the emphasis on courses has led many LEAs and voluntary organisations to overlook the importance of alternative vehicles for staff training and development'. (para 7.2.11.)[2]

In *A Framework for the Initial and Continuing Education and Training of Youth and Community Education Officers*[3] it was suggested that training for youth officers might be delivered in a number of different ways. As well as courses, there should be support, performance appraisal systems, planned experiences, preparation for transition and personal development opportunities.

It has already been said that training means more than just courses. Courses are, however, an effective and efficient method of training and must not be discounted in a full programme of learning. Course-based training allows students to meet other people with similar learning needs, it makes the best use of scarce training resources and gives time away from the everyday work to allow more objective consideration of ideas. It will be most effective where the course planners and the students have clear understanding about the aims and expected outcomes of the course at the outset. Courses may take students away from their working environments to be with people from other agencies or fields of work or they may be organised for all the staff of one workplace or agency in order to clarify and improve working practice. This latter method, called unit-based training, is increasingly being undertaken since it is more likely to bring about change in organisational style and practice.

In addition to more structured training and development activities, there is an immense training potential in support from colleagues. The characteristics of such support are that it will be actions and styles of behaviour which promote confidence and allow the person to question and evaluate his or her work in a non-threatening way. The support may be of a personal or professional nature and may take the form of helpful comment, team meetings, or more systematic approaches such as non-managerial supervision. The advantage to the individual officer are that, unlike most training courses, support may be on-going and applicable at all stages. The employing agency will appreciate the facts that it does not remove the officers from their work for long periods and that it costs little except for the time of other staff in short amounts.

There are many kinds of support which are relevant at every stage of an officer's career. Feed-back on performance and praise for good work is an important and often under-used form of support. The preparation of, and discussion about, references is another opportunity to give confidence. The role of professional associations in supporting officers is particularly important. It gives the opportunity to meet with colleagues and discuss work in a wider forum than the employing agency and with people of varying experience who have no hierarchical relationship with the officer. This may be particularly valuable to those officers in voluntary organisations which tend to have fewer staff. Likewise the practice of non-managerial supervision, in which a professional worker/officer engages in a non-judgemental, work-based discussion with another in order to examine and develop professional skill, has enormous training potential at every stage of career. Supervision of this kind should not be confused with informal chats with friends and colleagues, which may nevertheless be helpful. Rather, it is a structured process in which both the supervisor and supervisee have a clear and shared understanding about their respective obligations.

An understanding of group dynamics tells us that cohesion in a group increases with the frequency of its meetings. Regular meetings of officers within a team are likely to have this effect and to reinforce the confidence of individuals. It will also provide opportunities for checking out policy and styles of operation amongst fellow team members so that the individual officer, when confronted with problems in the field, will have greater personal authority, knowing what support may be available from his or her officer reference group.

Performance appraisal is the process of periodic assessment of a worker's performance in relation to the tasks he or she is engaged to carry out. It should be based upon a mutually agreed expectation of performance between the worker and the supervisor, and should be a joint assessment by the two of the worker's performance level. From a training viewpoint it has the advantage of identifying training needs, giving feedback and support and an opportunity to consider future developments and career prospects. Many organisations have adopted performance appraisal systems which allow every worker to enjoy the potential benefits of such assessment and which often result in far better training opportunities since there is constant focus upon the training needs within the organisation.

The work programme of youth and community officers tends to be seen in terms of what is necessary to perform their present tasks. Whilst acknowledging this requirement it may be that careful attention to activities would indicate opportunities for a progressive extension of experience which would not only enhance their present performance but would prepare them for future tasks. Training by means of planned opportunities offers practical experience as well as insight into future roles. The process by which this might happen entails setting objectives about those future states and then an examination of work programmes to see how opportunities might be identified and used. If particular areas of required skill were identified then one would look for opportunities in the officer's current duties to extend experience and competence in those areas. The 'shadowing' of, or substitution for a more experienced officer is one way in which this extension of experience will occur.

This shadowing process can bring benefits to the shadowed person as well as to the apparent student. John Mann, Director of Education in Harrow, wrote recently:

> I was suprised how much I got out of being shadowed. I was suddenly much more aware of the many different kinds of relationships my work involves ... I cannot commend shadowing too highly. I learned a lot, and may even have worked more effectively than usual, without losing a minute. Shadowing is indeed one of the most cost-effective and enjoyable of all forms of personal development.[4]

Chances for senior staff to undertake outside consultancy work with smaller agencies or colleges will also offer challenges which can extend the officer's skill. A more drastic step, but one recognised for its value, is job-swapping, which is especially appropriate for the established officer. Not only does this extend the officer's skill and provide a welcome variety of work, but in large organisations it can enhance inter-departmental relations and aid communications too.

Another under-used form of in-service training is the planned programme of reading. One of the disadvantages of being a manager in a large organisation is the amount of reading material constantly filling one's in-tray. Most managers have some system for reading or discarding such items, but tend to operate in this reactive way. Some time spent on planning a programme of reading to ensure that the manager increases and extends knowledge in priority areas in a more proactive manner will surely pay dividends in future situations.

Induction training, whilst commonplace, varies from an introduction to key individuals to a well-planned course of training over several weeks or months with explicit objectives and some evaluation of effectiveness. The INSTEP *Guidelines to a Staff Development Policy*[5] gives some suggestions for induction training in youth work. Perhaps of equal use to managers in the service is the recent publication by the Local Government Training Board and the Society of Education Officers entitled *The Training and Development of New Education Officers*.[6]

A comprehensive programme of training should include some attention to the social and interpersonal aspects of work and the personal development needs of the officer. In a service which is essentially concerned with the personal development needs of its users it is even more important not to neglect this need amongst its professional staff. To do so would increase the likelihood of unhappy and unbalanced staff whose work performance will be affected by their own unhappiness. The objectives of personal development training should include refreshment, recreation and successful interpersonal relationships for the individual worker. It is easy to minimise the importance of personal development opportunities because of the many demands upon time and money, but the employing agencies should regard as a legitimate training aim the enhancement of the officer's development as a person. It might be argued that all kinds of training can only benefit in a personal way. The particular emphasis here is on training which may not be directly related to the officer's post but which will undoubtedly enrich his or her professional life and which will certainly extend the repertoire of skill and understanding brought to the job.

The forms of personal development training which will be common throughout the officer's career include adequate time for reading and reflection and proper attention to holidays and time off. The history and nature of youth work mean that there is a high degree of voluntaryism and so the professional worker is often under pressure to neglect these important aspects. It is also necessary to foster personal interests in groups away from the work situation for self-enrichment and to preserve an independent view and perspective.

All of the different forms of training outlined above are necessary and legitimate parts in a comprehensive programme of in-service training. Attention to just one mode of training will impoverish the whole programme. Managers and their employers must be encouraged to view in-service training not as a series of 'one-off' events but as a continuous process of servicing which enables managers to maintain their peak level of efficiency and effectiveness.

Another common mistake is to assume that all recipients of training are the same. It is generally accepted that illiterate adults should not be taught to read and write using the same materials and techniques as for primary school children. The education has to be 'age-appropriate'. In the same way adults, even in similar jobs, will be at different stages of career, have vastly different length and variety of experience in those jobs and have different learning styles and capacity for new knowledge and skills. The training therefore has to take into consideration all of these differences and offer a variety of opportunities and styles which are appropriate to the trainees.

From the different ways of delivering training and the identification of various career stages a matrix of methods and stages can be constructed to form a framework of training opportunities for youth and community education officers. This framework provides a useful basis to consider how best the training can be achieved. It offers a starting point for officers themselves, employing agencies and regional and national training agencies to prepare training programmes in a more comprehensive and effective manner.

How can it be achieved?

The case for better training for youth service managers has been well made in a number of surveys and reports on the service. It is not enough simply to ask for better training. Neither is it enough for groups and agencies to be willing to offer training. Like most areas of public services the youth service has to compete for its resources with other legitimate bidders. What is needed to achieve the improved training is a campaign of both promotion and provision.

The responsibility for promotion should be undertaken by various bodies which can be identified. At national level the Department of Education and Science has responsibility for the quality of youth service provision and this is done by Her Majesty's Inspectors of Education. The recently established National Advisory Council for the Youth Service should support any moves to achieve better training opportunities. The Council for Education and Training in Youth and Community Work (CETYCW) has already identified the need through its joint publication referred to earlier[3]. Through its In-Service Training and Education Panel (INSTEP) the Council might ensure that officer training becomes a priority of its work. On behalf of employing agencies the National Council for Voluntary Youth Services and the local authorities should be pressing for improvement.

There has to be an agreed and recognised entitlement to time off for in-service training. The employer needs to ensure that the demands of the job and the way in which it is organised mean that this allocation of time is used and that it is not just a theoretical exercise. Adequate funding has also to be made available. A training budget of about three per cent of the total salary is a reasonable target figure for in-service training in order to capitalise most effectively on the investment of staff. Many local education authorities and voluntary organisations have prepared staff development policies for their youth and community services. Such policies must apply to officers as well as to other field-work staff.

The local authority associations could encourage member organisations to make available the resources and to establish structures which ensure that officer training happens. Since the majority of managers in the youth service probably work for local authorities it is surprising that the Local Government Training Board has not been more concerned with training for youth officers. The Society of Education Officers, in conjunction with the LGTB, produced a manual for the training of new education officers and it would be helpful to see this interest extended to cover youth service officers too. Finally, the National Association of Youth and Community Education Officers needs to give some priority to the achievement of better training for youth officers.

Provision of training will need to be done at various levels – nationally, regionally and locally. The Department of Education and Science has a programme of short courses and has a history of running longer courses from time to time. It is probably best placed to provide courses which are needed at national level for managers in the youth service.

In addition to the DES provision, training at national level could be done by various training agencies. Those colleges which offer initial and advanced training for full-time youth and community workers may be willing and able to provide in-service training for officers if the funding arrangements could be agreed. Many other institutions, such as polytechnics and universities, offer management training and courses in continuing education. Given adequate financial resources it should not be difficult to make provision on a national basis.

Regional training is an attractive prospect. Given sufficient demand for training within any region it is possible to provide non-residential courses or other forms of training which can be sustained over longer periods. It is also at regional level that officers from voluntary organisations and local authorities have the best opportunities for sharing in training provision.

At local level a good deal of the responsibility for training must lie with the individual managers. They must seek out and take advantage of training opportunities and take the initiative for personal study and support from colleagues. They are only likely to do this if their employers have created the right climate and circumstances within which this can occur.

The youth and community service has an immense task in equipping young people with adequate social and political skills to prepare them for adulthood. The present generation of adolescents face more difficulties than their parents, in many ways, and the role of the youth service is more vital than ever. Thus the service needs first-class managers.

So what will you do to ensure that your own training needs are met?

References

1. The Thompson Report (1982), *Experience and Participation, the Report of the Review Group on the Youth Service*, (para. 9–39) Command 8686, HMSO.
2. HMI Wales, (1984), *Youth Service Provision in Wales*, HMSO.
3. (1986), *A Framework for the Initial and Continuing Education and Training of Youth and Community Education Officers*, CETYCW/ NAYCEO.
4. Mann, J (1986), With my Shadow in Harrow, *Education*, 168 (17), 361.
5. INSTEP (1985) *Guidelines to a Staff Development Policy*, CETYCW.
6. *The Training and Development of New Education Officers*, Local Government Training Board and Society of Education Officers.

Appendix

Addresses of organisations referred to in Chapter 6

British Film Institute
81 Dean Street
London W1

Charity Commission (Liverpool)
Graeme House
Derby Square
Liverpool L2 7SB

Charity Commission (London)
14 Ryder Street
St. James's Square
London SW1Y 6AH

Commission for Racial Equality
Elliot House
10–12 Allington Street
London SW1E 5EH

Council for Educational Technology
3 Devonshire Street
London W1N 2BA

Department of Education & Science
Elizabeth House
York Road
London SE1 7PH

Department of Health & Social Security
Alexander Fleming House
Elephant and Castle
London SE1 6BY

Equal Opportunities Commission
Oversea House
Quay Street
Manchester M3 3HN

Health Education Authority
78 New Oxford Street
London WC1A 1AH

Health & Safety Executive
St. Hugh's House
Stanley Precinct
Bootle
Merseyside L20 3QY

Inland Revenue
Claims Branch
St. John's House
Merton Road
Bootle
Merseyside L69 9BB

Institute of Personnel Management
IPM House
Camp Road
Wimbledon
London SW19 4UW

Local Authorities Conditions of Service Advisory Board
41 Belgrave Square
London SW1X 8NZ

Music Publishers' Association
103 Kingsway
London WC2B 6QX

National Advisory Unit for Community Transport
Keymer Street
Beswick
Manchester M11 3FY

National Union of Teachers
Hamilton House
Mabledon Place
London WC1H 9BD

National Council for Voluntary Youth Services
Wellington House
29 Albion Street
Leicester LE1 6GD

National Youth Bureau
17–23 Albion Street
Leicester LE1 6GD

Performing Right Society Ltd
Copyright House
29 Berners Street
London W1 4AA

Phonographic Performances Ltd
Ganton House
14 Ganton Street
London W1V 1LB

Index

191